LIVING STRINGS

LIVING STRINGS

An Introduction to Biblical Spirituality

Michael Whelan, SM, PhD

E. J. DWYER

First published in 1994 by
E.J. Dwyer (Australia) Pty Ltd
3/32-72 Alice Street
Newtown NSW 2042
Australia
Ph: (02) 550 2355
Fax: (02) 519 3218

National Library of Australia
Cataloguing-in-Publication data

> Whelan, Michael, 1947 July 30- .
> Living Strings.
>
> Bibliography.
> Includes Index.
> ISBN 0 85574 373 5.
>
> 1. Bible—Criticism, interpretation, etc. 2. Spiritual life—Biblical teaching. 3. Spiritual life—Christianity. 4. Christian life—Biblical teaching. I. Title.
>
> 248.4

Copy-edited by Jean Cooney
Cover design by Michael Killalea
Text design by Warren Penney
Typeset in Goudy Old Style 11/14 pt by Egan Reid Ltd, NZ
Printed in Australia by Griffin Paperbacks, Netley, S.A.

10 9 8 7 6 5 4 3 2 1
98 97 96 95 94

Distributed in Canada by:
  Meakin and Associates
  Unit 17
  81 Auriga Drive
  NEPEAN, ONT K2E 7Y5
  Ph: (613) 226 4381
  Fax: (613) 226 1687

Distributed in the United States by:
  Morehouse Publishing
  871 Ethan Allen Highway
  RIDGEFIELD CT 06877
  Ph: (203) 431 3927
  Fax: (203) 431 3964

Distributed in Ireland and the UK by:
  Columba Book Service
  93 The Rise
  Mount Merrion
  BLACKROCK CO. DUBLIN
  Ph: (01) 283 2954
  Fax: (01) 288 3770

Thus did the Word of God,
who is David's son yet David's Lord,
play the song of the Spirit,
not on a lifeless harp,
but on the body and soul of man.
Thus did He make His music heard
through all the world.
On these living strings
He makes melody to God.

(Clement of Alexandria, c.150–215)

ACKNOWLEDGMENTS

The author gratefully acknowledges the use of material from the following works. Every effort has been made to locate the sources of quoted material and to obtain authority for its use.

From *The Search for God at Harvard* by Ari Goldman. Copyright © 1991 by Ari Goldman. Reprinted by permission of Times Books, a division of Random House, Inc.

From *The Philosophy of Paul Ricoeur* by C. E. Reagan & D. Stewart. Copyright © 1978 by C. E. Reagan & D. Stewart. Reprinted by permission of Beacon Press.

From "A Portrait of Dostoievsky", by G. Sigaux, Foreword to *Crime and Punishment* by F. Dostoievsky, J. M. Dent & Sons, date unknown, pp.x–xi.

From *Flowers in the Desert* by Demetrius Dumm. Copyright © 1987 by D. Dumm. Reprinted by permission of Paulist Press, publisher.

From "The Daemonic: Love and Death" by R. May. Reprinted with permission from *Psychology Today*. Copyright © 1968 (Sussex Publishers, Inc.).

The Scripture quotations in this publication are from the Revised Standard Version of the Bible, copyrighted 1971 and 1952 by the Division of Christian Education of the National Council of the Churches of Christ in the USA, unless otherwise indicated.

From *Report to Greco* by Nikos Kazantzakis. Copyright © 1973 by Faber & Faber, Ltd and Mr Patroclos Stavrou.

Reprinted by permission of Farrar, Straus & Giroux, Inc.: Excerpt from "The Enigma is Not Solved" from *God in Search of Man* by Abraham Joshua Heschel. Copyright © 1955 by Abraham Joshua Heschel, renewed © 1984 by Sylvia Heschel; excerpt from "Notes For A Philosophy of Solitude" from *Disputed Questions* by Thomas Merton. Copyright © 1960 by the Abbey of Our Lady of Gethsemani, renewed © 1988 by the Trustees of the Merton Legacy Trust.

From *The Revolt of the Masses* by Jose Ortega y Gasset. Copyright © 1932 by W. W. Norton & Company, Inc. Copyright renewed 1960 by Teresa Carey. Reprinted by permission.

CONTENTS

INTRODUCTION

When your words came I devoured them: Your word was my delight and the joy of my heart. (Jer. 15:16)

If you make my word your home you will learn the truth and the truth will make you free. (Jn. 8:32)

The word of God is something alive and active: it cuts like any double-edged sword but more finely: it can slip through the place where the soul is divided from the spirit, or joints from the marrow; it can judge the secret emotions and thoughts. (Heb. 4:12)

PREAMBLE

This book is primarily about Christian spirituality. Since Christian spirituality finds in divine revelation an ultimate reference point, the book is also about the Bible. The Bible will be pondered and discussed, not as an object of exegesis or critical research, but as a light that brings human existence into clearer focus, a Word of love spoken by a personal God, a sober challenge that calls illusions and counterfeits into question, a story that tells of God's search for us and our search for God.

The central aim of the book will be *to promote a growing sense of Scripture as revelation in daily living.* Too easily—often as the result of faulty spirituality—we develop the distorted view that "religion" stifles life. With all its rules and regulations it is, allegedly, incompatible with true freedom and joy. Implicit in this view is the denial of sacred Scripture as *revelation.* Scripture is implicitly seen, rather, as something added, some alien—and perhaps hostile—structure *imposed upon* human existence. And it may even be thought—perhaps inevitably—that this imposition originates in a capricious and judgmental "God."[1]

The Bible *exposes* rather than *imposes.* It is an unveiling, an uncovering, a bringing to light and setting free of *what is already there*, at least potentially. The Bible helps us to see "what is," to distinguish reality from irreality. The Bible reveals God as God really is, people as people really are, events as events really are, things as things really are—if we have the ears and eyes with which to hear and see. As the Hasidim say: "God dwells wherever man lets Him in."[2]

The revealing and the unveiling are in the oriental manner, by way of "pointing". The Bible bears some resemblance to the Zen koan in which the master, by stories, silences, actions, questions, paradoxes and the like, offers the student the opportunity of enlightenment. Much depends on the student's ability to "let go" and be willing to see things anew. A *change of consciousness* is crucial both in the receiving and in the results of the receiving.

A QUESTION OF CONSCIOUSNESS

By "consciousness" I mean the "mind-set" or taken-for-granted way of processing our interactions with people, events and things that is the continuing result of a constellation of factors—personality type, cultural, family and other life experiences giving rise to certain expectations, assumptions, thought patterns, inner conflicts, fears, anxieties and so on. For the sake of simplicity we can refer to it as *a particular way of thinking about and perceiving the world*.

Typically, the consciousness or mind-set of the biblical authors and their contemporaries is significantly different from the consciousness or mind-set of the Western reader of the Bible at the end of the twentieth century. Until we face this radical fact any approach to the Bible will be seriously deficient. In order to begin entering the world of the Bible we must first become aware of the world of human consciousness, especially our own.

There are at least five notable sociohistorical factors helping to shape the consciousness of the Western reader of the Bible today: (a) Greek philosophy; (b) the Schoolmen of the twelfth century; (c) the Reformation of the sixteenth century; (d) the Enlightenment of the seventeenth century; (e) affluence and consumerism.

(a) When confronted with the task of reflecting on the biblical revelation and explaining it to their contemporaries, the early Christian authors—including those in the New Testament—turned quite naturally to the Greek philosophical language and concepts, particularly as found in Plato (428–328 BC) and further developed in Neoplatonism by people such as Plotinus (205–70). While this was helpful, it carried with it certain disadvantages, one of them being the vulnerability to thinking in a non-biblical way about the biblical revelation.

In the first place, Greek thought carried the seeds of a certain *dualism* that was foreign to the Bible. In the second place, Greek thought about "perfection" and "holiness" tended to emphasize "the mind"—as opposed to "the passions"—and "flight of the alone to the Alone" ("monos pros monon") culminating in some final "achievement" or "end product" as the ultimate expression of human existence here and now. This tended to dispose Christian spirituality to move away from the biblical emphasis on the primacy and concreteness of human relationships.[3]

(b) The Schoolmen of the twelfth century tended to shift theological thought away from direct biblical reflection with lived reality in focus, towards discussion of theological tracts with abstract truth in focus. For the generations of Christians that followed, the Bible tended to become more and more remote from lived reality. Directives for living tended to come more and more from abstract thinking.[4]

(c) The Protestant Revolt or Reformation saw, among other things, the development of a climate of what may be termed "anti-thought." The Protestants were "anti" the current trend of tending to bypass the Bible. Luther called for a Christian life and theology that looked to "scriptura sola"—"scripture alone". The reaction from Rome was to emphasize the authority of the institutional Church and the role of the sacraments in opposition to the Protestants. The result was—in both Protestant and Catholic circles—a perception of the Bible that lacked adequate appreciation for its relevatory role in the ongoing life of the ecclesial community. The former tended to overlook the fact that the Bible is a dynamic revelation to be taken in dialogue with successive generations of the Christian faithful under the guidance of the Spirit. The latter tended to overlook the fact that it is the Word that calls the Church into existence and provides Her with the foundations of direction in every generation.[5]

(d) The Enlightenment saw the beginnings of the dominance of the "rationalistic" mind-set. "Dare to know!" was the catch phrase of this era. The older views of human existence and the world, frequently grounded in lack of knowledge, began to crumble in the face of the multiplication of the sciences. Holding the world and natural forces in awe tended to be replaced by the desire to master nature and bring its forces under control. In the wake of this evolution we have tended, among other things, to develop an unrealistic faith in the rational mind and a certain lack of faith in the poetic or mythological mind. In its extreme form, this kind of consciousness tends to accept as true only that which can be "proved" as fact. In other words, if the mind cannot—or does not as yet—understand or explain some phenomenon, it is to be shunned. Myths, legends, stories and the like tend to be relegated to the realm of the unsophisticated, the primitive, the unenlightened and so on. Although we may not accept this extreme view, we are nonetheless tainted by its influence. Typically we find it difficult to feel at home with myths and stories as valid modes of communicating truth. Yet, the biblical consciousness is not shaped by the Enlightenment and rationalism. It is much more at home with legends and myths, much less concerned with "factual" detail.[6]

(e) The affluent society, grounded as it is in a consumerist mentality, must also be considered. The availability of material comforts and the expectation that we "should" somehow possess these can take hold of our minds. Life's agenda can be set in such a way as to confuse the deeper and more lasting values unveiled in the sacred Scriptures.[7] In particular, the sense of "entitlement" to material things can be radically at odds with what the Sacred Scriptures are revealing to us and asking of us.[8]

IN SEARCH OF BIBLICAL CONSCIOUSNESS

The following characteristics of the biblical writings may help us to continue working towards a greater empathy with the biblical consciousness. In the first place, "the central thought of Judaism is the living God."[9] Consciousness of the transcendent-immanent God who has chosen this people permeates every part of the Bible. The authors are captivated by that Reality and all their thoughts, reflections, descriptions of people, recordings of events and perceptions of things take for granted the presence and influence of the living God. They could never think of themselves, other people, events or things except in relationship to the living God. We might say theirs is a "transcendent consciousness." Or, more precisely, they are a people in whom the trans-conscious—that openess of the human consciousness to "the more than," "the beyond," "the divine"—is very alive. For them the sacred is the profane, the profane is the sacred.

In the second place, "biblical religion starts with events."[10] The biblical mind focuses on what is happening or has happened before it considers who is involved—verbs precede subjects.[11] Subjects find their significance in terms of the events they are caught up in—and life is made up of a never-ending series of interconnected events. History is pre-eminently *salvation history*, a history of God's liberating action. God is the God-who-acts. We might say theirs is a "process-oriented consciousness."

For them life is constant "event" (from the Latin "e" and "venire," "to come out" or "to show forth") a constant epiphany of the living God.

In the third place, the Bible is at home with paradox. It is in touch with the Real beyond the real that can only be pointed to and creatively struggled with if we relinquish the desire for clear definitions. The Jewish teachers knew that stories generally revealed more of the truth than definitions. Jesus, so much attuned to this consciousness, gave his disciples parables to ponder rather than rules to follow or dogmatic formulae to learn.[12]

The Bible can hold up David and Peter as paradigms of fidelity at the same time as it talks quite frankly of their gross infidelities. It can speak of the unutterably transcendent God at the same time as it speaks of God's deep compassion for a chosen people among whom he has "pitched his tent." The Bible can speak of dying in order to live, being blessed when you are poor and persecuted. The Bible can do this because it presumes the limits of the human mind and its language and takes for granted that human existence is a wonderful absurdity, a tragic triumph of God's loving hand, a call to something more than the human heart can possibly imagine.

In the fourth place, the Bible is thoroughly immersed in time even as it is timeless. The faithful disciple who wants to read the Bible with an open mind and heart, intent on hearing the Word, must experience himself or herself as part of the drama that the Bible is. Abraham Heschel writes that "the Bible is not a book to be read but a drama in which to participate."[13] The Bible will not be a source of life for me if it remains simply an object of academic or aesthetic interest, or a collection of rules and moral norms, or a factual record of what has happened and what will happen. I must experience what is written there as intimately expressive of my own life.

Elie Wiesel expresses the subtlety and depth of this disposition towards the Bible when he speaks of the one who must tell the biblical stories. It applies just as well to the one who is to listen to those stories:

> Disciple more than anything else, his aim is not to plunge into historical exegesis—which surely lies beyond his competence—but to reacquaint himself with the distant and haunting figures that moulded him. He will try to reconstruct their portraits from Biblical and Midrashic texts, and eventually insert them into the present.
>
> For Jewish history unfolds in the present. Refuting mythology, it

affects our life and role in society. Jupiter is a symbol, but Isaiah is a voice, a conscience. Mars died without ever having lived, but Moses remains a living figure. The calls he issued long ago to a people casting off its bonds reverberate to this day and we are bound by his Laws. Were it not for his memory, which encompasses us all, the Jew would not be Jewish, or more precisely, he would have ceased to exist.

Judaism, more than any other tradition, manifests great attachment to its past, jealously keeping it alive. Why? Because we need to. Thanks to Abraham whose gaze is our guide, thanks to Jacob whose dream has us spellbound, our survival, prodigious on so many levels, lacks neither mystery nor significance. If we have the strength and the will to speak out, it is because every one of our forebears expresses himself through us; if the eyes of the world often seem to be upon us, it is because we evoke a time gone by and a fate that transcends time. *Panim* in Hebrew is used in the plural form: man has more than one face. His own and Adam's. The Jew is haunted by the beginning more than by the end. His messianic dream is tied to the kingdom of David and he feels closer to the prophet Elijah than to his next-door neighbor.

What is a Jew? Sum, synthesis, vessel. Someone who feels every blow that ever struck his ancestors. He is crushed by their mourning and buoyed by their triumphs. For they were living men and women, not symbols. The most pure, the most just among them, knew ups and downs, moments of ecstasy and confusion; we know, for they are described to us. Their holiness was defined within human terms of reference. Thus the Jew remembers them and sees them as they were at the crossroads of their own lives: troubled, exalted, marked. They are human beings: people, not gods. Their quest rejoins his own and weighs on his decisions. Jacob's ladder rends his nights. Israel's despair burdens his solitude. He knows that to speak of Moses is to follow him to Egypt and out of Egypt. To refuse to speak of him is to refuse to follow him.[14]

AN EXERCISE IN THINKING

The French philosopher Paul Ricoeur notes an underlying structure to the parable of the treasure in the field[15] and suggests that it may be a useful paradigm in understanding the parables as such.[16] The parables, he argues, appeal to the imagination rather than the will. Only when we have been "put in motion" by the insight into reality that the parable bears, can we turn our minds and hearts to action. The Event-Reversal-Decision structure Ricoeur finds in the parables can also give us a practical format for developing our own consciousness in tune with the Bible:

Step One—*"Event"* (*"The Finding"*): Take a certain passage from the Bible and read it meditatively, with a keen ear to what is happening to you as you do so. Wait upon the text. Allow it to affect you. Chew over particular words and phrases. (This may take say 5 to 15 minutes.) Then take pen and paper and simply express what is beginning to move within yourself. Do not worry about sentence construction or grammar. Still with a keen ear to what is happening within you gently try words, phrases, images that may fit the inner movements. It may go something like this: "I feel . . . funny . . . a sort of hollow feeling . . . yes, empty . . . sad . . . Sad about what? . . . life in general . . . I remember when I was seven . . . I can see myself there in the backyard . . . Anyone else there? . . . no . . . I used to play by myself a lot and . . . yes, Dad used to do a lot of traveling . . . Mum and I were home by ourselves most of the time . . . How does that seven year old feel there in the backyard? . . . etc." Let it run, listening attentively, asking questions that flow out of what has already surfaced. Let the experience have a life of its own. Keep going until there is some sense of completion. (This may take, say, 30 to 40 minutes—though do not feel bound by this time frame.)[17]

Step Two—*"Reversal"* (*"The Selling"*): Leave the writing at this point and gently consider what has emerged. Does it point to any "baggage," obstructions to the fullness of life, any lack of freedom? Stay with that. Let it come home to you in the context and mood set by the Mystery being revealed through the Word. Simply face that "baggage," dishonesty, anxiety, obstruction or lack of freedom, hold it up to God. Make a decision to stand against it without resolving to willfully rid yourself of it. Perhaps your journey entails carrying that baggage for sometime yet. Leave it in God's hands. Humbly face the truth that has emerged. (This may take, say, 5 or 10 minutes—though do not feel bound by this time frame.)

Step Three—*"Decision"* (*"The Buying"*): Gently consider yourself and your life in the light of what has emerged to this point. Is there something in particular you would like to affirm, give thanks for, say "yes" to? Dwell with that, allow it to make its home in you just a little more deeply. Again there is no question of willfully striving to make anything happen. It is more a question of resting with God in the presence of something good, savoring a contemplative moment. Conclude with a brief prayer of thanksgiving and perhaps petition. (This may take, say, 5 to 10 minutes—though do not feel bound by this time frame.)

Notes

For all titles mentioned in the text and notes, full bibliographic information is provided in the Bibliography on pp 181ff.

1 This perspective is probably more common in the West than we care to admit, although it may be disguised under words such as "righteousness," "God's will," "eternity," "moral integrity," "principle," "orthodoxy," etc. In such cases the rhetoric belies an insidious counterfeit to a genuinely biblical spirituality.

2 M. Buber 1958, p.176. The complement to this is Karl Barth's observation that biblical revelation is the opening of a door that can only be unlocked from the inside (cited by Thomas Merton. Cf. Thomas Merton 1966, p.18).

3 Cf. A. Heschel 1975, p27ff. In another place Abraham Heschel notes: "Geographically and historically Jerusalem and Athens . . . are not too far removed from each other. Spiritually they are worlds apart." (A. Heschel 1978, p.15; cf. whole section in this book, 3–23.) Cf. also R. Schnackenberg 1968, p.160ff. See also W. Barrett 1958, pp.69–148.

4 Cf. F. Vandenbroucke, "New Milieux, New Problems" in L. Bouyer n.d., pp.223–9. One of the positive features of the Protestant Revolt of the sixteenth century was a desire to return to the Word. Thus, this criticism applies more to the Roman Catholic tradition than to the Reformed tradition.

5 Compare your own experience and what you learned about the Bible with that outlined in the teaching of the Second Vatican Council, especially in "Dogmatic Constitution on Divine Revelation" ("Dei Verbum"). For example: "The People of God is gathered into one first of all through the word of the living God" ("Decree on the Ministry and Life of Priests," n.4); "The Church has always venerated the divine Scriptures just as she venerates the body of the Lord, since from the table of both the Word of God and the body of Christ she unceasingly receives and offers to the faithful the bread of life, especially in the sacred liturgy" ("Dogmatic Constitution on Divine Revelation," n.21).

6 Cf. H. Smith 1978, for an excellent discussion of the typical characteristics of the modern consciousness and its roots. Cf. Also M. Whelan, "Formative Mind I" in Christian Life Formation, Part Two, Lecture Nine—Audio Cassette and Notes (Daughters of St Paul, 1985). The difference in thinking may be highlighted by a simple reference to the Book of Judith. As one commentator notes: "(The) presentation of Nebuchadnezzar, the Babylonian, as king of the Assyrians, waging war against Arphaxad, an unknown Median king, with an army commanded by the Persians Holofernes and Bagoas, is the equivalent of saying that Peter the Great, King of England, waged war against Arphaxad, the king of France, with an army led by Generals Eisenhower and MacArthur." (P. F. Ellis 1963, p.523) The biblical author has no problem with this. The twentieth century, rationalistic reader does have some problems though!

7 Cf. J. Kavanaugh 1981, and E. Fromm 1976. C.S. Lewis comments in The Screwtape Letters, "Prosperity knits a man to the world. He feels that he is 'finding his place in it.' While it is finding its place in him" (p.143). Walker Percy comments: "The consumer of mass culture is lonely, not only lonely, but spiritually impoverished" (Walker Percy 1991, p.302). The writings of Walker Percy are highly recommended as a complement to this book. In this context, Percy's Lost in the Cosmos: The Last Self Help Book, is worth special mention.

8 Early in the sixties, American author Daniel Boorstin wrote The Image, or What Happened to the American Dream which began in the following way: "I want to describe the world of our making, how we have used our wealth, our literacy, our technology, and our progress, to create the thicket of unreality which stands between us and the facts of life . . . We (Americans) expect too much of the world. Our expectations are extravagant in the precise dictionary sense of the word'—going

beyond the limits of reason or moderation.' They are excessive. When we pick up the newspaper at breakfast, we expect—we even demand—that it bring us momentous events since the night before. We turn on the car radio as we drive to work and expect 'news' to have occurred since the morning newspaper went to press. Returning in the evening, we expect our house not only to shelter us, to keep us warm in winter and cool in summer, but to relax us, to dignify us, to encompass us with soft music and interesting hobbies, to be a playground, a theater, and a bar. We expect our two-week vacation to be romantic, exotic, cheap, and effortless. We expect a faraway atmosphere if we go to a nearby place; and we expect everything to be relaxing, sanitary, and Americanized if we go to a faraway place. We expect new heroes every season, a literary masterpiece every month, a dramatic spectacular every week, a rare sensation every night. We expect everybody to feel free to disagree, yet we expect everybody to be loyal, not to rock the boat or take the Fifth Amendment. We expect everybody to believe deeply in his religion, yet not to think less of others for not believing. We expect our nation to be strong and vast and varied and prepared for every challenge; yet we expect our 'national purpose' to be clear and simple, something that gives direction to the lives of nearly two hundred million people and yet can be bought in a paperback at the corner drugstore for a dollar. . . . . Never have people been more the masters of their environment. Yet never has a people felt more deceived and disappointed. For never has a people expected so much more than the world could offer." (Cited by W. Lynch, 1965, 258f)

9   A. Heschel 1975: p.25.
10   Op. cit.: p.16f.
11   Cf. D. Dumm 1987: pp.22–34.
12   Cf. for example, Jan Lambrecht writes:
     "It is precisely because a parable is a sort of 'kill-joy' or an irritant in a sense that it possesses a thought-provoking power. It appeals to the reflective capacities of the hearers. It obliges them to ask themselves why such a story is being told at this point. It is normal that the hearer will want to examine more closely, will wish to understand, what appears to be odd. Then whenever the insight after an initial resistance suddenly breaks through, whenever the clouds of the image are penetrated by the light of meaning, whenever a 'disclosure' occurs, then the hearer recognizes with full certainty that the concrete situation has been illuminated and explicated by the parable. German exegetes rightly state . . . 'The parable explains, but cannot itself be explained', as one could explain, e.g., a similitude or an allegory. Once the enigmatic parable has been understood, it takes hold of its hearers; it has convinced them. They perceive the connection between image and reality. They acknowledge the parable's message. The evidence becomes luminous and the complex, obscure situation itself has become much more transparent and clear. David has to acknowledge that Nathan is right: 'I have sinned against the Lord'" (2Sam 12:13) 1981, p.4.
13   Heschel 1976, p.254. See also Bernhard Anderson 1990. This is a revision of a much earlier work designed to introduce people to "the drama of the Bible" through study groups. It has much to recommend it.
14   Wiesel 1976, pp.xi–xiii.
15   Cf. Mt. 13:45f.
16   Cf. P. Ricoeur 1978. This little essay is reproduced as Appendix A.
17   E. Gendlin 1986, may offer a useful aid in this step.

1
DIVINE WORDS

On the mountain, from the heart of the fire, Yahweh spoke to you face to face, and I stood all the time between Yahweh and yourselves to tell you of Yahweh's words, for you were afraid of the fire and had not gone up the mountain. (Ex. 5:4f–JB)

This God, his way is blameless; the word of Yahweh is without dross. (Ps. 18:30–JB)

In the beginning was the Word: the Word was with God and the Word was God. . . . The Word was made flesh. (Jn. 1:1 & 14–JB)

THE WORD IN THE CHRISTIAN COMMUNITY

In this chapter we continue our process of "working back" from our experience of words—their use and abuse—through the Christian community's experience of *the Word*, towards *the biblical proclamation of the Word*. Grace builds on nature. God speaks a divine, eternal Word that is expressed through a human, finite word. We gain access to that world of the Word which is God's revealing and healing conversation with the human family through the word that is part of our everyday existence.

The Second Vatican Council gives us a good perspective on the Word in the community, even if that perspective is not always successfully expressed by and embodied in the community:

The People of God are gathered into one first of all through the Word of the living God.[1]

The Church has always venerated the divine Scriptures just as she venerates the body of the Lord, since from the table of both the Word of God and the body of Christ she unceasingly receives and offers to the faithful the bread of life, especially in the sacred liturgy.[2]

Among the principal duties of the bishops, the preaching of the Gospel occupies an eminent place.[3]

Only by the light of faith and by meditation on the Word of God can one always and everywhere recognize God in whom 'we live, move and have our being' (Acts 17:28).[4]

Christian husbands and wives are co-operators in grace and witnesses of faith on behalf of each other, their children and all others in their household.[5]

A love, veneration, and near cult of the sacred Scriptures lead our brethren to a constant and expert study of the sacred text. For the Gospel is 'the power of God unto salvation to everyone who believes, to Jew first and then to Greek' (Rom. 1:16).[6]

In the liturgy we find evidence of this teaching concerning the centrality of the Word as a life-giving dynamism in the community. Every time the community gathers for worship, it is the Word that is called upon to give meaning and direction to that gathering. This happens most obviously in the celebration of the sacraments, but also in other liturgical and para-liturgical events. The liturgy of the Eucharist gives special emphasis to the Word, where the proclamation of the Gospel in particular is seen as the presence of Christ Himself.[7] The new rite of the Liturgy of Reconciliation begins with a reading from the Word of God to set the context for that celebration.

The Fathers of the undivided Church in their writings demonstrate a profound respect for the Word.[8] For the Fathers, "the Word of God is like another Incarnation or the assumption of a new form by the eternal Logos."[9] "The Word is another and complementary form of the Eucharist."[10] "The Word of God is life-giving and comparable to Baptism."[11] "The Word of God effects the forgiveness of sins in the manner of the sacrament of penance."[12] "In its twin forms the Logos reveals the new, higher dignity of man and a fresh concept of the world."[13] "The Word of God also constitutes the family as a church within the Church."[14]

The Desert Fathers generated an interesting custom. They were seen as people who lived in fidelity to the Word and were therefore special channels of the Word's wisdom. People would come to them and ask for "a word" for light and life. For example: "A certain brother went to Abbot Moses in Scete, and asked him for a good word. And the elder said to him: 'Go, sit in your cell and your cell will teach you everything.'"[15]

THE WORD IN THE BIBLE[16]

The Bible makes one of the most startling and ultimately incomprehensible claims: It is the Word of God! The eternal, transcendent-immanent God uses the words, signs and symbols of the finite human family to speak to us. Thus, the Word of God is more than an object of abstract speculation—just as the word of loving spouses or friends is more than an object of abstract speculation. It is rather an expression of God, a manifestation of the relationship God has chosen to form with the people. God reveals and acts in the Word.[17]

In the Bible the Word is always in the context of two key events: the Exodus and Covenant of the Old Testament (OT) and the Passover of Jesus—the new Exodus and new Covenant—of the New Testament (NT). In the OT, nothing is written before the Exodus event and everything is written in the light of the Exodus event, God loving this people into freedom. In the NT, nothing is written before the Passover of Jesus and everything is written in the light of the Passover of Jesus, God bringing that freedom to fruition through his incarnate Word. The intentionality of the Word in the Bible is clear: *to reveal and effect the ultimate freedom of creation.*[18]

Any word of truth, love, wisdom, power, comes ultimately from God. Note the recurrence of phrases in the OT—particularly in the Prophets—reminding the people of that origin of the Word: "Yahweh is speaking" (Is. 1:2); "it is Yahweh who speaks" (Joel 2:12); "This is the word which came to Jeremiah from the Lord" (Jer. 21:1); (as a prelude to the Decalogue and setting the context for that set of laws) "I am Yahweh your God" etc. (Ex. 20:1ff.).

The Word is a memory, a power to recall the great event of liberation when God called the people forth in the desert to speak to them and lead them in his ways of love. It is a revealing and healing conversation that is eternal, ever old, ever new, always beckoning us into a loving relationship where we will find our true freedom. This "Yahweh who speaks" is the God who acts, the living, liberating God. To forget this fact is to lose contact with the life-giving power of the Word. The Word carries the people's very identity. If they should ever cease to listen to that Word they would cease to exist. The Word connects them with the saving Mystery and the healing mercy at the heart of that Mystery by allowing them to live in the experience of being loved into freedom. Disconnected from this Word, Judaic religion and morality are reduced to ritualism and legalism.

In the NT the intentionality is the same but the phraseology is different. The eternal Word, enfleshed in Jesus of Nazareth, has passed from death to life and lives in the community. There is more confidence and clarity in referring to this Word. "The Word was made flesh and dwelt amongst us" (Jn. 1:14); "Make your home in my word, you will learn the truth and the truth will set you free" (Jn. 8:31f.); "the word of the Lord continued to spread" (Acts 6:7); "the word of God is something alive and active" (Heb. 4:12). Again the Word is an efficacious memory, a powerful recall that can connect us to the Christ event. Disconnected from that event of liberation it loses its meaning, and again, Christian religion and morality are reduced to mere ritualism and legalism.

The liberation revealed and effected through the Word is ultimately a liberation from sin and all its manifestations.[19] The Word not only reveals the true nature of the human condition as "fallen"[20]—and therefore crying out for liberation—it is, in fact, the only possibility of genuine freedom.[21] Truth, born of communion with the Word, "will make you free."[22]

Clearly, the "factual" words of the purely rationalistic mind are too limiting to fulfil the purpose described above. Unlike ours, the Hebrew mind moves easily beyond the "factual" and empirically verifiable. Its use of words reflects this: mythology, metaphor, paradox, symbol, poetry, legend and apparently "wild stories" are part and parcel of Hebrew language and ways of describing the world, of expressing experience of the Real. They know the rational mind is far too constricting to handle any but miniscule pieces of reality at a time. They are not embarrassed to leave mere rationality behind and launch into the transrational.

For the rationalistic among us this presents a serious problem: we identify myth—and these other instruments of human communication—with "unreality" and the "irrational," allowable perhaps for the un-educated and the unsophisticated, but certainly not permissible for any sophisticated contemporary person who thinks at all.

In actual fact these uses of language imply a humble recognition of the limits of the human mind and its consequent inability to adequately name what it is grappling with. Mythological language takes us to the borders of thought and says "Look beyond! Wonder, and contemplate the incomprehensible mystery of it all!". In a discussion of the mythologies of various cultures, one author comments:

> Myths are serious stories that reflect a society's spiritual foundations. They are symbols of human experience that each culture values and preserves because they embody the worldview or important beliefs of that culture. Myths may explain origins, natural phenomena, and death; they may describe the nature and function of divinities; or they may provide models of virtuous and heroic behavior by relating the adventures of heroes. They may include legends as well as folklore. They impart a feeling of awe for whatever is mysterious and marvellous in life, depicting a universe in which human beings take their place in a much larger scheme.[23]

The principal obstacle to our encountering truth in myths is our own limited consciousness. Myths are potentially vehicles of truth just as authentic as any other use of words may be.

OUR COMMUNION WITH THE WORD OF THE BIBLE

One simple and practical manifestation of the revealing and effective quality of the Word has already been indicated through the "Exercise in Thinking" outlined above.[24] Engaging the Word in faithful and humble meditation can bring us face to face with our evasions and illusions, the issues of life that stand between us and the next phase of the journey to which the Spirit calls us. What is more, there is power in this moment of revelation as we commune with the Word. We are enabled by grace to let go and move on, entering more deeply into the Mystery through the Word. The words of Rainer Maria Rilke might apply to one who meditates the Word with a view to absorbing it: "He does not always remain bent over the pages; he often leans back and closes his eyes over a line he has been reading again, and its meaning spreads through his blood."[25]

The Christian assembly summoned by the Word is—today at least—something of a problematic forum for communion with the Word. As a society in general (in the West), genuine ritual and festivity, leisure and play, seem to be somewhat alien to us. We find it difficult to express ourselves in these forms. Perhaps they only come with depth of authentic culture, that is when the structures of human society are developed in openess to the transcendent. As a Christian society in particular, communal worship presents serious difficulties. There are many differing expectations from the participants, few accepted rituals that have the power to lift us out of the distracted routines of the here-and-now, and even fewer(?) pastors and preachers who can make sense of the Word and celebrate it in a meaningful way. The comment of Martin Luther on preachers of his day seems pertinent to our own:

> This is the way it has gone with preaching . . . after the text of the Gospel is read, they take us to fairyland. One preaches from Aristotle and the heathen books, another from the Papal decretals. One brings questions about his holy water, another about blue ducks, another about hen's milk. . . . In short this is the art in which nobody sticks to the text from which people might have had the Gospel.[26]

Plus ça change, plus c'est la même chose. Yet it must certainly be a source of serious concern to us that men and women who have gone through a supposedly thorough preparation for ministry, a preparation supposedly quite sophisticated and learned, cannot effectively celebrate and proclaim the Word.

What is happening? Perhaps we—as individuals and especially as proclaimers of the Word—do not know how to engage the Word in the kind of revealing and healing conversation indicated above? Perhaps we are unwilling to do that for fear of what it may ask of us? Perhaps it is not possible to consistently and effectively celebrate and worship only in large groups? Perhaps our noisy and distracted lifestyles have lost touch with the power of solitude and silence?[27]

Whatever the precise causes of the problems besetting worship in the Christian assembly, there does seem to be some value in promoting individual communion with the Word as indicated above and partici-pating in smaller study and prayer groups where deeper issues can be engaged, explored and meditated on at some length and depth.[28]

Two individuals from the Bible stand out as offering some leads on the above questions: Jeremiah and Paul. For both of these individuals the Word is definitely something "alive and active," a Mystery that has taken hold of their very beings. Jeremiah endeavoured to escape his vocation because he did not like proclaiming "violence and ruin" and being "the laughing stock" of the people. Yet he was "caught":

> You have seduced me Yahweh and I have let myself be seduced; you have overpowered me: you were the stronger. . . . I used to say, 'I will not think about him, I will not speak in his name any more.' Then there seemed to be a fire burning in my heart, imprisoned in my bones. The effort to restrain it wearied me, I could not bear it. (Jer. 20:7–9 –JB)

Paul implies a similar experience of the Word when he writes:

> I have not yet won, but I am still running, trying to capture the prize for which Christ Jesus captured me. (Phil. 3:12)

PRACTICAL SUGGESTIONS

(a) Meditate on the liturgy of the Word for either one of the weekdays or a coming Sunday. What would you say to the people in your family/community/parish by way of a homily arising out of those texts? Perhaps you could begin by doing the "Exercise in Thinking" outlined above.[29] You might prefer to follow the suggestions for preparing a homily outlined in Appendix B. Or you might prefer to make up a story that communicates the message emerging from the sacred text. Whatever you do, meditate on the texts first with a view to what they mean to *you* before you start thinking about what you might tell *others*.

(b) Set aside some time(s) in the coming week—say 20 minutes each—and practice the art of "spiritual reading" and "meditation" with a chosen text of Scripture.[30]

Notes
1 "Decree on the Ministry and Life of Priests," n.4.
2 "Dogmatic Constitution on Divine Revelation," n.21. See also the rest of this Chapter VI. It is interesting to note that St Thomas Aquinas calls preaching "*officium principalissimum sacerdotis*"—"the principal duty of the priest."
3 "Dogmatic Constitution on the Church," n.25.
4 "Decree on the Apostolate of the Laity," n.4.
5 "Decree on the Apostolate of the Laity," n.11.
6 "Decree on Ecumenism," n.21. Cf. also A. Bea, "The Bible in the Life of the Church" in *A New Catholic Commentary On Holy Scripture*, Nelson 1969, pp.3–13.
7 Note the words of the minister of the Gospel before and after the proclamation and the responses of the assembly: The minister begins with a silent prayer before the book of the Gospels, "Cleanse my heart and my lips that I may worthily proclaim your holy Gospel,"then says "The Lord be with you" and the people respond "And also with you." The focus is an interchange between the minister and the people. The minister then signs the book of the Gospels with the sign of the cross saying, "A reading from the holy Gospel according to . . ." and the people respond "Glory to you Lord." At this point the focus has shifted quite explicitly to the Lord. Minister and people then both sign themselves with the sign of the cross on the forehead, lips and heart. At the end of the Gospel the minister proclaims "This is the Gospel of the Lord" and the people respond "Praise to you, Lord Jesus Christ." Clearly the proclamation of the Gospel is seen as *the very presence of the Lord in the midst of the community*. The homily which follows and reflects on the proclaimed Word thus has great significance in the Christian assembly. Cf. Second Vatican Council "Dogmatic Constitution on Divine Revelation," n.25 and "Constitution on Sacred Liturgy," n.52.
8 Cf. L. Bopp 1964, pp.147–67; also D. Rees 1969 pp.14–20.
9 L. Bopp, op. cit., p.148.
10 Op. cit., p.149.
11 Op. cit., p.155.
12 Op. cit., p.156. Note: The minister who proclaims the Gospel bows toward the book of the Gospels and prays "May the words of this Gospel wipe away our sins." We can presume that the expectation of the community is that this prayer will be effective.
13 Op. cit., p.161.
14 Op. cit., p.164.
15 T. Merton 1970, p.30. Note: There were no Bibles available to the people at this time. The Canon of Scripture only began to take some definite shape with the African Councils at the end of the fourth century. Which books should in fact be included within the Canon of Scripture is still not resolved within the Christian community at this time. What is more, the printing and multiplication of available texts was very limited during those centuries prior to the invention of the printing press in the middle of the fifteenth century. (Gutenburg printed the first Bible on a

press in 1453.) People relied on the oral tradition and on the preaching of those who did have access to texts. Memorization of particular texts was common and in fact was a central feature of the Desert Fathers and their heirs, the monks, who "munched" on chosen words from Scripture as they went about their work. A whole prayer style—thoroughly grounded in Scripture—emerged at this time. The "Jesus Prayer" is perhaps the best example of it though there are others. Cf. L. Bouyer n.d., pp.376 and 510.

16 Cf. For example, X. Leon-Dufour 1967, pp.585–9; *The Interpreter's Dictionary of the Bible*, Volume 4, Abingdon, 1962, pp.868–72); T. Maertens 1964, pp.11–12.

17 Cf. For example Gen. 1:3ff: "And God said, 'Let there be light'; and there was light".

18 Cf. Rom. 8:18–27 and Gal. 5:1–12.

19 Cf. Rom. 5:12–21: "Therefore as sin came into the world through one man and death through sin, and so death spread to all men because all men sinned—. . . But the free gift is not like the trespass. For if many died through one man's trespass, much more have the grace of God and the free gift in the grace of that one man Jesus Christ abounded for many."

20 Cf. Gen. 3:1–13: ". . . So when the woman saw that the tree was good for food, and that it was a delight to the eyes, and that the tree was to be desired to make one wise, she took of its fruit and ate; and she also gave some to her husband, and he ate." Cf. also Rom. 5:12–14 already noted above.

21 Cf. For example Acts 4:12: "And there is salvation in no one else, for there is no other name under heaven given among men by which we must be saved."

22 Cf. Jn. 8:32: ". . . and you will know the truth, and the truth will make you free."

23 D. Rosenberg 1986, xiv.

24 Cf. p.17. See also Martin Smith 1989. Smith has some excellent practical suggestions for prayerful meditation on the Scriptures.

25 Cited by C. Cummings 1984, p.9.

26 Source unknown. Consider the observation of a contemporary author: "What are the causes of the de-Christianization of our present-day world? Canon Boulard, following Abbé Godin, emphatically asserts that the greatest blame is to be borne by inadequate preaching. At one and the same time, our teaching has lacked the realism and the forcefulness of the Gospels. The 'inquest' points an accusing finger at a *crisis*: a lack of confidence in the Word of God as an instrument of the coming of the Kingdom. It is now a commonplace to denounce a type of worship which has become sclerotic for lack of proclaiming the Good News. It would be perhaps more in order to fear the opposite risk: so much insistence on preparing the soil that the result is a distrust of preaching. If there is one point on which Christian thinking should examine itself, it is that of the *role of the Word in building up the Church*." (Y. B. Trémel 1964, p.171.

27 "One can hear silence sounding through speech. Real speech is in fact nothing but the resonance of silence." Max Picard 1957, p.27. Walker Percy suggests three particular obstacles in the listeners: "The first is a consumership mentality, a bland but nonetheless tenacious addiction to the diversions of the media and the manifold goods and services of a technological society. . . . Another idol, even more subtle in guise, is the growing fascination with what can only be called the occult, the magical. . . . sustained by an insatiable appetite for the superficially mysterious, it mistakes religion for its own credulity towards such things as astrology, the Bermuda Triangle, UFO's, reincarnation, this or that guru with self-appointed mystical powers. . . . And a third force . . . the new fundamentalists. . . . In my opinion, they do a disservice by cheapening the vocabulary of Christianity and pandering to a crude emotionalism divorced from reason." Walker Percy, "A 'Cranky Novelist' Reflects On The Church" 1991, pp.322f.

28 For a good discussion of this problem, see Dominic Grasso 1965, pp.ix–xxxiii.

29 Cf. p.17.
30 For a guide to "spiritual reading" and "meditation" in the Christian tradition see
    Aelred Squire pp.117–27; Michael Whelan 1986, Chapters 20, 21 and 22; Adrian
    Van Kaam 1976, pp.125–52; Guigo II 1978, pp.81–99; G. Martin 1975; Chiara
    Lubich 1975; Susan Muto 1976.

2
COVENANT

I will remember my covenant which is between me and you and every living creature of all flesh; and the waters shall never again become a flood to destroy all flesh. (Gen. 9:15)

When Israel was a child, I loved him, and out of Egypt I called my son. (Hos. 11:1)

And he took bread, and when he had given thanks he broke it and gave it to them, saying, "This is my body which is given for you. Do this in remembrance of me." And likewise the cup after supper, saying, "This cup which is poured out for you is the new covenant in my blood." (Luk. 22:19f.)

HUMAN RELATIONSHIPS

Before we start to speak about the meaning of Covenant as a theological reality, we would do well to reflect on the human reality which gives rise to its language and imagery. And I am not talking primarily about the language and imagery of "covenants" in the laws and customs of the peoples of biblical times. I am talking about *human relationships*. Central to the very nature of the human person *qua* person is relationship. We cannot conceive of ourselves except in relationship. We are always "towards" others.

One obvious reason for any society to sanction and encourage marriage, in some form or other, is procreation. But we are more than brutes. We seek more than biological ends when we seek out a partner. We seek completion as a person, expression of our very being as a person. Part of the mystery of love is that each of us is given the gift of self through the love of another. What are we if we have never loved or been loved? Can we love if we have not first been loved by another? By our very natures we seek relationships in the full sense of that word as a *sine qua non* for genuinely human existence.

Such is our need and our desire. But in this fallen condition, the need and the desire are problematic. Relationships lead us into here and now reality, not paradise. Relationships, like life itself, are tragicomic affairs. Peter Sellers was particularly adept at portraying this. Pullitzer Prize winning author Jane Smiley captures it well in the following piece from one of her novels. Clare, a more than middle aged aunt, whose husband has died, talks with Christine, her young niece, who has been married for one year and is thinking of a divorce:

> If you're thinking about this proposed divorce, Christine, I have something to say about it, too. And I have a right to say it, because I've watched you grow up, and I've loved you and cared for you almost as much as your mother and grandmother have, so if you think it's interfering, then so be it. I'm going to interfere. You made your choice. You had lots of dates in high school and college, and Todd was the one you wanted. You knew him as long as I knew your uncle Geo and longer than your mother knew your father. You had time to think about his peculiarities and about the life it seemed like he was going to lead. You knew that changing him was unlikely, because I heard your mother say something about that to you, and I heard you say that you'd take him as he is. I heard that! Now things don't seem to be going your way, and you want to get out. You think you can make another choice, one that won't demand as much accommodation or sacrifice. Well, you're wrong. Let me tell you, none of our lives has turned out the way we thought it would, or wanted it to. If the preacher had said during my wedding, 'Clare, do you take this man to worry about money with, to have miscarriages with, to argue about childraising with, to lose in middle age,' do you think I would have said yes? Of course not! When I was twenty three I wanted your uncle Geo to be rich and healthy and happy, always handsome like he was then. But that's not life and marriage is life! You know what getting married is? It's agreeing to taking this person who right now is at the top of his form, full of hopes and ideas, feeling good, looking good, wildly interested in you because you're the same way, and sticking by him while he slowly disintegrates. And he does the same for you. You're his responsibility now and he's yours. If no one else will take care of him, you will. If everyone else rejects you, he won't. What do you think love is? Going to bed all the time? Poo! Don't be weak. Have some spine! He's yours and you're his. He doesn't beat you or abuse you, and you've made about the same bargain. Now that you know what it's like to be married, now that all the gold leaf has sort of worn off, you can make something of it, you can really learn to love each other.[1]

It is tempting to idealize relationships—especially those with an erotic dimension. However, the idealizing can only occur if it is accompanied by denial and evasion. The idealizer seeks an idol, not a person, the satisfaction of some inner wish, not self-transcendence. The idealizer engages in monologue, not dialogue.[2]

The Jewish philosopher Martin Buber has analyzed human relationship insightfully in his classic book *I and Thou*. Buber argues that we find our fullest expression as persons in an "I/Thou" relationship. We recognize the other as "person"—"Thou"—and are recognized in turn as "person"—"Thou." In such an experience the "in between" becomes all important. An "I/Thou" relationship requires self-transcendence, each must "go out" towards the other in self-forgetfulness. There is nothing paradisiacal or magical here. Nor is there anything instantaneous. There is, though, effort, generosity, forgiveness, trust, fidelity, mercy and compassion. There must be. If there is not, the "Thou" slips away easily into "You," and the "You" slips away easily into "It."

COVENANT AS RELATIONSHIP

Covenant in the Bible may be understood as the fullest expression of personhood—ours and God's. God seeks relationship. Indeed, there is a frightening truth embedded in the story of the Covenant: *God needs us!* Frightening because it is metaphysically absurd. God *cannot* need us. Yet it seems from the biblical portrayal, that God is like us: incomplete without relationship. The Bible story of the Covenant speaks of a loving, personal Mystery, who simply could not leave us in our folly. Nowhere is this better revealed than in Hosea:

> When Israel was a child, I loved him, and out of Egypt I called my son. (2) The more I called them, the more they went from me; they kept sacrificing to the Ba'als, and burning incense to idols. (3) Yet it was I who taught E'phraim to walk, I took them up in my arms; but they did not know that I healed them. (4) I led them with cords of compassion, with the bands of love, and I became to them as one who eases the yoke on their jaws, and I bent down to them and fed them. (5) They shall return to the land of Egypt, and Assyria shall be their king, because they have refused to return to me. (6) The sword shall rage against their cities, consume the bars of their gates, and devour them in their fortresses. (7) My people are bent on turning away from me; so they are appointed to the yoke, and none shall remove it. (8) How can I give you up, O E'phraim! How can I hand you over, O Israel! How can I make you like Admah! How can I treat you like Zeboi'im! My heart recoils within me, my compassion grows warm and tender. (9) I will not execute my fierce anger, I will not again destroy E'phraim; for I am God and not man, the Holy One in your midst, and I will not come to destroy. (10) They shall go after the Lord, he will

roar like a lion; yea, he will roar, and his sons shall come trembling from the west; (11) they shall come trembling like birds from Egypt, and like doves from the land of Assyria; and I will return them to their homes, says the Lord.[3]

The Covenant relationship is unique however. It is the liberating, redemptive relationship between the transcendent-immanent God and the chosen people. Through the chosen people that redemptive relationship becomes one with all humanity. The liberating and redemptive qualities we find in any genuinely loving relationship is merely a faint reflection of this primordial loving relationship. No other relationship holds out the possibilities this one does. God invites us into a divine communion, as one author puts it:

> God wishes to lead all to a life of communion with Himself. It is this idea, fundamental to the doctrine of salvation, which the theme of the covenant expresses. In the OT it dominates all religious thought, but we see it deepen with the passing of time. In the NT it acquires an unparalleled fullness, for henceforth it has as its content the total mystery of Jesus Christ.[4]

THE ROOTS OF THE CONCEPT

In the OT, the word Covenant (*berit*) is "a term so rich it captures the heart of Israel's religious beliefs."[5] It tells of the divine election and the promises made, it is a gyroscope in the consciousness of the people, a compass in their journey as pilgrims through the ages, a seminal friendship they must never forget and to which they will be constantly recalled by the Law and the Prophets. This Covenant is concretized in the great event of the Exodus and recalled by the people in every subsequent event of exile and liberation to this day:

> Israel becomes Yahweh's covenant partner in response to His elective love; the dialogue of redemptive history continues. The covenant becomes the basis of Israel's relationship to God through historical events and sets her faith worlds apart from the religions around her, tied as they were to the cycle of nature, fertility cults, magical practices, and capricious divinities. Faithfulness was expected of a covenant partner. In the years and centuries ahead Israel would often be wanting in covenant loyalty (*hesed*), but was never abandoned by the God who called her. Israel's most frequent song of praise would be *"ki le'olam hasdo"*—"For his *hesed* is everlasting."[6]

The covenant is clearly seen in its reaffirmation with the people through Moses.[7] God's choice is one of pure grace,[8] given in love and promising freedom. The people, finding their identity in this gracious election, respond in faith and determine to live in fidelity to the relationship thus established. Ultimately the Law and the Prophets find their meaning in this Covenant—and only in this Covenant.[9] This same Covenant finds echoes in other "covenants" made with individuals.[10] The essence is always there: a gracious election has given rise to an unbreakable bond with commitments on both sides.

The Prophets foreshadow a new and everlasting Covenant.[11] This is an extension of the promise inherent in the primary covenant of Sinai. The great event of the Exodus is a symbol and pointer to a final liberation yet to be revealed.

In the Septuagint the word "berit" is translated by the Greek diatheke. "In the language of Hellenistic law this term designated the act by which one disposes of one's goods (will) or declares the provisions which he intends to effect."[12] The emphasis in this usage is on the authority and status of the person making the contract or will. Thus, in the Septuagint, Covenant brings into focus the divine transcendence and the graciousness of the action on the part of God.

The word diatheke is mentioned in the four stories of the Last Supper.[13] The Covenant of Sinai was sealed in the blood of animals.[14] The new Covenant is to be sealed in the blood of Jesus—God himself.[15] Jesus stands in the long tradition of the chosen people and their relationship with God. He reveals the fullness of that relationship in which the human family, and ultimately all creation, is to be set free. The ancient relationship, established with the first Covenant, does not end. It is clarified and confirmed. The people's pilgrimage with God thus does not end, it continues in the light of Christ and the power of his Spirit.

PRACTICAL INSIGHTS ARISING

The reality of the Covenant implies some practical insights for Christian life formation. In the first place, I recognize that life is marked by a certain "triangularity"—an ongoing relationship between God, self and the world of other people, events and things. The relationship with God—my primary relationship as creature—is revealed, confirmed, enhanced and enlightened, and forms the context for all relationships that are part of the structure of human existence in general and in particular. To think in only "vertical" or "horizontal" terms about the Christian life is to distort it. God has declared sacred forever that which lies at the heart of human existence—relatedness. Ultimately, the call to love, central to both the OT and the NT, is a call to recognize and creatively foster the interdependence between God, ourselves, each other and the created world in which we live.[16]

In the second place, I find my identity, and thus my purpose and meaning in life, just as the Church does, in and through the Covenant. Any thinking about myself, any choice of vocation, must be done in the light of this identity gained from God's choice of me in particular, and the pilgrim people in general. To lose sight of this in self-reflection will, typically, lead to introspection and a dislocated and unhealthily isolated view of the self. To lose sight of this when making significant life choices will lead us away from the sources of wisdom and energy that alone can see us through the morass of illusions and irrealities that beset every human journey. God's question to Adam—"Where are you?"[17]—is a radical question of identity addressed to all human beings. It embodies a challenge: Remember who you are, do not forget![18]

In the third place the relationship which God has graciously offered in the Covenant invites a free response from each of us—a decision. "See, I have set before you this day life and good, death and evil."[19] Jesus never forced himself upon the people.[20] The decision I make is continually renewed and remade in the light of my ongoing experience of the relationship. And the same applies to the Church—it must constantly submit itself to renewal, to conversion, to clarifying its purposes and choosing again and again to live in fidelity to the covenant.[21]

In the fourth place the three principal elements of the Covenant—grace, love and freedom—must characterize any genuine biblical spirituality or morality. Just as I, graciously chosen by God through no particular virtue of my own, am being loved into freedom, so I should behave that way towards the world. This presupposes that I constantly remember, reimmerse myself—through liturgy, communion with the Word and constant mindfulness of God acting in my life—in the reality of that relationship. Thus my behavior is marked by the consciousness of God's graciousness towards me, that all is gift, that I must work hard to affirm and foster the relatedness of life, that freedom for people, events and things to become what they are is paramount. There is a definite call here to acknowledge anxieties, insecurities and illusions that entrap and imprison me and others so easily.[22]

PRACTICAL SUGGESTIONS

a) The Book of Proverbs has a number of references to friendship. For example: "A friend loves at all times, and a brother or sister are born for adversity."[23] "There are friends who pretend to be friends, but there is a friend who sticks closer than a brother or sister."[24] "Faithful are the wounds of a friend; profuse are the kisses of an enemy."[25] Do you have a "friend"? What distinguishes this friendship from other relationships which you have?

b) Describe your relationship with God. (Use your journal or simply reflect on it, by yourself or with a friend.) What are the principal features of that relationship? Is it entirely honest? How has it changed over the years? How do you ensure that the relationship stays alive? Do you need to do anything at this time to deepen that relationship? Is this your primary relationship? How does it affect your other relationships?

c) In John's Gospel there are several places where Jesus refers to himself and his disciples as "friends": "Thus he spoke, and then he said to them, 'Our friend Lazarus has fallen asleep, but I go to awake him out of sleep.'"[26] "Greater love has no man than this, that a man lay down his life for his friends. (14) You are my friends if you do what I command you. (15) No longer do I call you servants, for the servant does not know what his master is doing; but I have called you friends, for all that I have heard from my Father I have made known to you."[27] Meditate on these texts and try to go deep into their significance. You might find it helpful to reflect in your journal as part of the meditation. You might also find it helpful to speak with a friend about these texts.

Notes
1 Smiley 1984, p.162f.
2 "Of the erotic life, Martin Buber has remarked that in no other realm are dialogue and monologue so intermingled and opposed. I would agree that any attempt to offer a normative description would have to include precisely such mingling and opposition. Even if we place it optimally within an ongoing domestic world of affection, in which sex bears some relation, however slight, to procreation, our task is still the difficult one of maintaining that sex is both utterly important and utterly trivial. Sex may be a hallowing and renewing experience, but more often it will be distracting, coercive, playful, frivolous, discouraging, dutiful, and even boring. On the one hand, it tempts man to omnipotence, while on the other, it roughly reminds him of his mortality. Over and over again it mocks rationality, only to be mocked, in turn, in the very instance it insists its domain is solely within the senses. Though it promises the suspension of time, no other event so sharply advises us of the oppressiveness of time. Sex offers itself as an alternative world, but when the act is

over and the immodesty of its offering is exposed, it is the sheer worldliness of the world we briefly relinquished and must now re-enter that has to be confronted anew. Residing no longer in the same room that first enclosed us, we lie now in another room with another topography—a room whose surfaces, textures, corners, and knobs have an otherness as absolute and formidable as the duties and promises that nag us with their temporal claims. What began as relief from worldly concern ends by returning us to the world with a metaphysical, if unsettling, clarity." (L. Farber 1976, 126f.)

3 Hos. 11:1–11.

4 Xavier Leon-Dufour 1967, p.75.

5 Cf. L. Boadt 1984, p.175. Cf. Also J. Jensen 1982, pp.82–6; B. Anderson 1975, pp.76–97; W. Buhlmann 1982, pp.11–62.

6 J. Jensen, op. cit., p.83.

7 "Then the Lord said, 'I have seen the affliction of my people who are in Egypt, and have heard their cry because of their taskmasters; I know their sufferings, (8) and I have come down to deliver them out of the hand of the Egyptians, and to bring them up out of that land to a good and broad land, a land flowing with milk and honey, to the place of the Canaanites, the Hittites, the Amorites, the Per'izzites, the Hivites, and the Jeb'usites. (9) And now, behold, the cry of the people of Israel has come to me, and I have seen the oppression with which the Egyptians oppress them. (10) Come, I will send you to Pharaoh that you may bring forth my people, the sons of Israel, out of Egypt.'" Ex. 3:7–10 Cf. Also Ex. Chs. 19–24 and 32–4).

8 "It was not because you were more in number than any other people that the Lord set his love upon you and chose you, for you were the fewest of all peoples . . ." Dt. 7:7.

9 Jesus' arguments with the Scribes and the Pharisees can be understood in this context—they had shifted the focus of the Law from being a means to fidelity to the Covenant to being an end in itself. Forgetfulness is the besetting sin of human institutions, including those that profess to be religious.

10 For example: ". . . and God remembered his covenant with Abraham, with Isaac, and with Jacob." Ex. 2:24 (JB).

11 For example: "And I will betroth you to me for ever; I will betroth you to me in righteousness and in justice, in steadfast love, and in mercy. (20) I will betroth you to me in faithfulness; and you shall know the Lord. (21) And in that day, says the Lord, I will answer the heavens and they shall answer the earth; (22) and the earth shall answer the grain, the wine, and the oil, and they shall answer Jezreel; (23) and I will sow him for myself in the land. And I will have pity on Not pitied, and I will say to Not my people, 'You are my people'; and he shall say 'Thou art my God.'" Hos. 2:19–23. Cf. Also Jer. 31:33 and 32:37–41; Ezek. 16:60, 34:23 and 36:26.

12 Xavier Leon-Dufour, op. cit., p.78.

13 "And he said to them, 'This is my blood of the covenant, which is poured out for many.'" Mark 14:24. Cf. Also Mt. 26:28; Lk. 22:20 and 1Cor. 11:25.

14 "And Moses took the blood and threw it upon the people, and said, 'Behold the blood of the covenant which the Lord has made with you in accordance with all these words.'" Ex. 24:8.

15 "And he took a cup, and when he had given thanks he gave it to them, saying, 'Drink of it, all of you; (25) for this is my blood of the covenant, which is poured out for many for the forgiveness of sins. (26) I tell you I shall not drink again of this fruit of the vine until that day when I drink it new with you in my Father's kingdom.'" Mt. 26:24-6.

16 "No man is an island entire unto itself; every man is a piece of the continent, a part of the main." (John Donne, "Devotions" xvii) For an explicit development of "relationship" as central to biblical spirituality see, for example, W. Dicharry 1985.

17 Cf. Gen. 3:9.
18 For a wonderful development of this theme, see Martin Buber 1966.
19 Dt. 30:15
20 "O Jerusalem, Jerusalem, killing the prophets and stoning those who are sent to you! How often would I have gathered your children together as a hen gathers her brood under her wings, and you would not!" (Lk. 13:34)
21 "The Church is an evangeliser, but she begins by being evangelised herself. She is the community of believers, the community of hope lived and communicated, the community of brotherly love; and she needs to listen unceasingly to what she must believe, to her reasons for hoping, to the new commandment of love." Paul VI, *Evangelii Nuntiandi*, n.15. Conversion will be discussed in greater detail in Chapter 12.
22 Concern for orthodoxy is legitimate, indeed necessary. Right teaching and right action go hand in hand. Yet excessive concern for orthodoxy, like excessive concern for anything, can lead us away from what really matters. Orthodoxy disconnected from the Covenant ceases to be orthodox. It becomes truth in the service of error.
23 17:17
24 18:24
25 27:6
26 Jn. 11:11
27 John 15:13–15

3
THANKSGIVING

Ascribe to the Lord the glory due his name; bring an offering, and come before him!
Worship the Lord in holy array; (30) tremble before him, all the earth; yea, the world
stands firm, never to be moved. (31) Let the heavens be glad, and let the earth rejoice, and
let them say among the nations, "The Lord reigns!" (32) Let the sea roar, and all that fills
it, let the field exult, and everything in it! (33) Then shall the trees of the wood sing for joy
before the Lord, for he comes to judge the earth. (34) O give thanks to the Lord, for he is
good; for his steadfast love endures for ever! (35) Say also: "Deliver us, O God of our
salvation, and gather and save us from among the nations, that we may give thanks to thy
holy name, and glory in thy praise. (36) Blessed be the Lord, the God of Israel, from
everlasting to everlasting!" Then all the people said "Amen!" and praised the Lord.
(1Chron. 16:29–36)

Bless the LORD, O my soul; and all that is within me, bless his holy name! (2) Bless the
LORD, O my soul, and forget not all his benefits. (Ps. 103:1f.)

And do not get drunk with wine, for that is debauchery; but be filled with the Spirit, (19)
addressing one another in psalms and hymns and spiritual songs, singing and making
melody to the Lord with all your heart, (20) always and for everything giving thanks in the
name of our Lord Jesus Christ to God the Father. (Eph. 5:18–20)

THE HUMAN EXPERIENCE OF GRATITUDE

The etymology of the English word *gratitude* is interesting. It is rooted in the Latin word *gratia* meaning *gift, favor* or *grace*. When we experience this disposition of *gratitude*, we typically *thank* the one who is the source of a gift, favor or grace of some kind. Our English word *thank* is rooted in our English word *think*. When I *thank* you I *think* of you in a kind, gracious way that acknowledges the gift, favor or grace that you have shared with me.

So what does the actual *experience* of gratitude imply? When I am *grateful*, when I *give thanks* what is happening? I might *say* things like: "Thanks," "Thank you very much," "That was generous of you," "I appreciate that" and so on. The language—let us presume for the moment that we are working within the bounds of sincerity—points to a very specific reality.

Firstly, it points to *relationship*. I thank *someone*. Another person (or persons) is involved. Secondly, the other person has *favored* me in some

43

way. By being present to me in some positive way, by acting for me, the other has been a source of gift, favor or grace. Thirdly, this calls me to *respond* in a similar vein, to think graciously of that other, to thank.

There is something creative going on in that relationship. The mutuality is being fostered. Something close to the core of what it means to be a person is affirmed. I am disposed to the other, and the other to me, in a positive, lifegiving way. Moments of genuine gratitude are moments of self-transcendence, where we meet each other "in between."

The ability to enter this kind of exchange, to be grateful, is one of the marks of a mature person. We teach children to say "Thank you." That does not make them grateful. It may help. But gratitude is a grace that is acquired slowly, subtly, sometimes painfully, like the other good qualities of life. Mostly we pick it up by moving in an atmosphere where gratitude is part of the air we breathe. By osmosis we learn to be grateful people. Or, more precisely, we learn to be grateful, and *in that* become mature persons.

Obviously, gratitude can be abused like any other human experience. Human relationships need to be redeemed. They manifest the flaws of fallen formation like the rest of our lives. I may bestow a favor—even that expression has certain negative connotations!—in order to establish an IOU that I can call on at another time. This is very much part of our social reality. It happens in the business world and amongst politicians. But it also happens in the family living room, between spouses, between children and their parents. We sometimes call it "love with strings attached." Mostly we do not call it anything.

On the other hand, I may *express* gratitude, *say* "Thank you!" but not *be* grateful. Just as the giver can bestow favors with ulterior motives, so the recipient can give thanks with ulterior motives. In both instances gratitude is being counterfeited. The genuine self-transcendence is lacking. It is, to use Buber's language, double monologue rather than real dialogue. Despite the appearances.

So where does that leave us? It leaves us in the same place as we are left when we consider any of the virtues. We recognize the ideal. We also recognize the human reality. Realistically speaking, perfect gratitude, like "perfect" anything in this fallen world, is not possible to us. Our best will always be a fallen best. But that is no reason not to continually apply ourselves to facilitating our openness to the grace of gratitude. Self-transcendence is the primary sign of human maturity. It is a lifetime's work. At the end of our lives we will, at best, be able to say "By the grace of God I tried very hard."

Something needs to be said of two characteristics that oppose gratitude and thanksgiving. In the first place there is *resentment*. Instead of simple straightforward gratitude to each other, we may experience tinges of resentment mixed with the gratitude—or even outright resentment with no gratitude at all. Resentment may emerge, for example, after repeated instances of abused mutuality in relationships. It may also emerge out of selfishness and a desire to avoid the demands of genuine human relationship which inevitably forces me up against myself.

If relationships are to be successful, we must render ourselves vulnerable.[1] To be invulnerable is to be non-relational in any human sense. When people allow themselves to be vulnerable they are likely to be hurt just as they will inevitably hurt others similarly disposed. That is life. That is also why the virtues need each other. We cannot be grateful unless we are also forgiving.

It may be that resentment becomes endemic to societies that are excessively individualistic. Thus, the second characteristic opposing gratitude is *individualism*.[2] Individualism resents social responsibility, being under obligation to another. Individualism therefore finds the genuine disposition of gratitude threatening, even degrading. Genuine gratitude necessarily moves towards communion. Individualism moves in the opposite direction, towards isolation and self-sufficiency. To be in a position where you are called to say "Thank you!" implies that you are dependent, or at least interdependent, and not self-sufficient. Genuine gratitude is not only a necessary basis for communion of persons, it is a forceful counter to individualism.

THANKSGIVING AND GRATITUDE IN THE BIBLE

A contemporary Orthodox Jewish writer gives us a good starting point for reflecting on gratitude as it is in the Bible:

> After the synagogue prayers on Saturday morning, the crowd descends to the social hall and stands chattering around the tables of food while waiting for the rabbi to say the *b'racha*, the blessing, on the wine so that everyone can begin. I grew up with these b'rachas, an essential part of the everyday life of an Orthodox youngster. *"Baruch atah Adonai Eloheynu Melech Ha'olam hamotzi lechem min ha'aretz,"* one says before eating bread. "Blessed are you God, King of the Universe, who brings

forth bread from the ground." There is another b'racha for vegetables ("... who brings forth the produce of the ground") and another for pastries ("... who created different kinds of cakes"). And then there is a whole different category—b'rachas that you say when you see lightning or a rainbow, b'rachas after recovering from an illness and, most routinely, a long laundry list of b'rachas in the daily prayers—giving thanks for waking up, for freedom, for new clothes, for the ability to study Torah—there is even one, recited by boys and men, thanking God for not making us women, and another, recited by males and females, praising God for not making us Gentiles. Upon leaving the bathroom, we make a b'racha thanking God for our internal plumbing system. In yeshiva, our rebbe taught us that "a good Jew" has to say one hundred b'rachas a day. My mother spent my childhood years on b'racha patrol, making sure that nothing would pass my lips without thanks to the Almighty properly expressed. After she gave me a cookie, she would watch closely for the mumble. Saying b'rachas is a habit that never left me, and it still sometimes looks like I am talking to my food before I pop it in my mouth. It is an involuntary act and, on those rare occasions when I think about what I am doing, I kind of like it. In the great scheme of things it seems only right to give thanks.[3]

The first reality of biblical history is the gift of God as God—unmerited, superabundant. This is, in its most radical form, what we call *grace*. The encounter with God does not put us simply in the presence of the Absolute; it *completes* us and *transforms* our lives. It gives us our very *identity*. This relationship is what we are ultimately made for. The revelation on Mt. Horeb points to this:

God said to Moses, "I AM WHO I AM." And he said, "Say this to the people of Israel, 'I AM has sent me to you.'" (15) God also said to Moses, "Say this to the people of Israel, 'The Lord, the God of your fathers, the God of Abraham, the God of Isaac, and the God of Jacob, has sent me to you': this is my name for ever, and thus I am to be remembered throughout all generations.[4]

Thanksgiving appears as the response to this progressive and continual *grace* which one day should blossom in Christ. At the same time there is an intense awareness of the manifold gifts of God throughout creation. This awareness gives us a spirit permeated with wonder because of God's generosity, a joyous recognition before the divine greatness.

Thus a disposition of thanksgiving is perceived as essential in the Bible because it is a fundamental religious reaction of the creature when he or she discovers, in a tremor of joy and veneration, something of God, of his greatness and of his glory. The capital sin of pagans, according to Paul, is "not to have rendered to God either glory or thanksgiving."[5] And, in fact, in the mass of hymns created by the piety of Mesopotamia, the sentiment of thanksgiving is rare; while it is very frequent in the Bible and evokes powerful outpourings of the soul.[6]

The theme of *thanksgiving* is a natural corollary of the Covenant theme. The English word *thanksgiving* fails to convey all the nuances and depth of the Hebrew words *"todah"*(from the root word *"yad,"* meaning *"hand,"* and *"yadah"* meaning *"open hand"*), which implies admiration and grateful confession of the wonders of God, and *berakah,*which implies an abundance of gratitude and appreciation. "Berakah" is normally translated as *"blessing."*

Todah and its cognates are found in some of the Psalms and Canticles of the OT.[7] *Berekah* and its cognates offer us a rich expansion of the reality of thanksgiving in the OT. It contains the recognition of "gift" and the fact that all "blessings/gifts" come from God and are an expression of God's benevolence.[8] "Blessings" intend the fulness of life which is ultimately God's gift.[9] The verb *to bless* (*barak*) has a wide range of uses— from a simple greeting[10] and the customary formula of courtesy[11] to the highest gifts of the divine favour.[12] It is the first duty of the creature "to bless" God.[13]

The participle *blessed* (*baruk*) is the strongest of all the words of blessing. This word is typically used as a spontaneous cry of recognition that God has poured forth his wondrous love in a special way.[14] Similarly the cry of blessing may be addressed directly to God.[15]

In the NT thanksgiving is typically found in the context of *confession* (*"homologeo"*)[16] *praise* (*"aineo"*),[17] *glorification* (*"doxazo"*),[18] and *blessing* (*"eulogeo"*).[19] A new expression, practically unknown in the OT, finds its way into the NT language of thanksgiving: "eucharistia" and "eucharisteo," "to be thankful" or "thank." The word and its cognates are used more than sixty times in the NT. *"Eucharistia"* in its original root meanings connotes "right/proper joy."[20] For the Christian, Jesus is the thanksgiving to the Father, and in the Last Supper he has given the community a thanksgiving meal to keep before our consciousness the great liberating Passover event and the New Covenant.[21]

PRACTICAL INSIGHTS ARISING

The theme of thanksgiving, as it comes through in both the OT and NT, carries some practical insights for Christian life formation. In the first place, the dominant reality in the Christian consciousness is to be the God who acts lovingly in this world and for this world. God is actively with and for us. The Christian life anchors itself in that awareness first and foremost. And that awareness engenders expressions of wonder and praise, joy and gratitude. To start our reflections on the Christian life with what *we* must do distorts the project because, psychologically, we tend to finish where we begin. The ecstasy[22] that is a normal development of this kind of consciousness focused on the God who acts, becomes impossible—can only be counterfeited—unless we are centred beyond ourselves.[23]

In the second place we can begin to understand something of St Paul's mindset when he says "All things work to the good of those who love God,"[24] and St Augustine's insight when he adds, "Yes, even our sins." Life is on our side, as it were, not agin us. It is basically promise, not threat. The consciousness permeated by gratitude is always open to opportunity. It blesses God in all things. No tragedy or disaster is ever seen as a totally closed and ultimate experience of evil. Evil there is, but it never has the last word. There is no room for cynicism in the Christian consciousness. "Rejoice always, pray constantly, give thanks in all circumstances."[25]

In the third place our ability to relate creatively with people is enhanced in this environment of thanksgiving. It is the possibilities in people—rather than their impossibilities—that we search for and are alert to. Perhaps one of the most damning things that happens to people along the journey of life is that they are "cursed" rather than "blessed" by those they encounter. One of the promising signs in the Church's understanding of mission and evangelization at this time is her willingness to "bless" individuality and such enriching possibilities as may be found, for example, in culture and personal experience. To fail to recognize this in those with whom we wish to share the Good News is, in a sense, to "curse" rather than "bless" them. What a difference it would make to our encounters with people if we approached them with the expectation of being touched by the wonders of God through them, rather than simply presuming that we already possess the wonders of God which we are about to impose on them.

PRACTICAL SUGGESTIONS

(a) Pay attention to prayer at meal times this week. Grace before and after meals is as much a blessing *of* God as it is a request for a blessing *from* God. (The very word "Grace" implies that the food is "gift" for which we give thanks.)

(b) Make a point, this week, of being alert to people, events and things around you. Open your eyes—inner and outer eyes—and look! Allow reality to come to you, to speak to you, to reveal itself to you. Allow the pure graciousness of the life that is given to you to become even more real for you through this receptivity and alertness to what is happening around you. Watch and bless!

(c) When you next celebrate the Eucharist, pay close attention to the Eucharistic prayer. *Hear* the words. Pay particular attention to the words of consecration and what they imply, intend and recall in our rich Judaeo-Christian tradition.

(d) Pray for someone who has hurt you, or perhaps someone whom you simply do not like. Invoke God's blessing on them as God sees fit.

Notes

1   The English word *vulnerable* comes from the Latin *vulnus* meaning *wound*. The vulnerable person is, literally, one who is able to be wounded. Needless to say, there is only so much wounding any person can take.

2   Individualism is a deformation of healthy individuality. True human community cannot be formed without individuality. That is, people must regard themselves as accountable and take responsibility for themselves as adult human beings.

3   Ari L. Goldman 1991, p.14f.

4   Ex. 3:14-15

5   Rom. 1:21 (JB)

6   Cf. X. Leon-Dufour 1967, p.525.

7   For example: "I wash my hands in innocence, and go about thy altar, O Lord, (7) singing aloud a song of thanksgiving (*todah*), and telling all thy wondrous deeds." Ps. 26: 6-7 "O give thanks (*yadah*) to the Lord, call on his name, make known his deeds among the peoples! (9) Sing to him, sing praises to him, tell of all his wonderful works! (10) Glory in his holy name; let the hearts of those who seek the Lord rejoice! (11) Seek the Lord and his strength, seek his presence continually! (12) Remember the wonderful works that he has done, the wonders he wrought, the judgments he uttered, etc." 1Chr 16:8–12

8   "Blessings (*berakah*) are on the head of the righteous, but the mouth of the wicked conceals violence. . . . (22) The blessing (*berakah*) of the Lord makes rich, and he adds no sorrow with it." Prov. 10:6 and 22

9   Note Jacob's testament to his twelve sons which includes a special blessing for Joseph: "Joseph is a fruitful bough, a fruitful bough by a spring; his branches run over the wall. (23) The archers fiercely attacked him, shot at him, and harassed him sorely; (24) yet his bow remained unmoved, his arms were made agile by the hands of the

Mighty One of Jacob (by the name of the Shepherd, the Rock of Israel), (25) by the God of your father who will help you, by God Almighty who will bless (*barak*) you with blessings (*berakah*) of heaven above, blessings (*berakah*) of the deep that couches beneath, blessings (*berakah*) of the breasts and of the womb. (26) The blessings (*berakah*) of your father are mighty beyond the blessings (*berakah*) of the eternal mountains, the bounties of the everlasting hills; may they be on the head of Joseph, and on the brow of him who was separate from his brothers." Gen. 49:22–6

10 "He said to Geha'zi, 'Gird up your loins, and take my staff in your hand, and go. If you meet any one, do not salute (*barak*) him; and if any one salutes (*barak*) you, do not reply; and lay my staff upon the face of the child.'" 2Kg. 4:29

11 "Then Joseph brought in Jacob his father, and set him before Pharaoh, and Jacob blessed (*barak*) Pharaoh. (8) And Pharaoh said to Jacob, 'How many are the days of the years of your life?' (9) And Jacob said to Pharaoh, 'The days of the years of my sojourning are a hundred and thirty years; few and evil have been the days of the years of my life, and they have not attained to the days of the years of the life of my fathers in the days of their sojourning.' (10) And Jacob blessed (*barak*) Pharaoh, and went out from the presence of Pharaoh." Gen. 47:7 and 10

12 "The Lord has greatly blessed (*barak*) my master, and he has become great; he has given him flocks and herds, silver and gold, menservants and maidservants, camels and asses." Gen. 24:35

"Hast thou not put a hedge about him and his house and all that he has, on every side? Thou hast blessed (*barak*) the work of his hands, and his possessions have increased in the land." Job 1:10

13 "Ever since the creation of the world his invisible nature, namely, his eternal power and deity, has been clearly perceived in the things that have been made. So they are without excuse; (21) for although they knew God they did not honor him as God or give thanks to him, but they became futile in their thinking and their senseless minds were darkened." Rom. 1:20-1 (Cf. Also Dan. 3:57–88—found in the Apocrypha.)

St Augustine is one who knew the truth of St Paul's vision: "And what is this? I asked the earth, and it said, 'I am not he!' And all things in it confessed the same. I asked the sea and the deeps, and among living animals the things that creep, and they answered, 'We are not your God! Seek you higher than us!' I asked the winds that blow: and all the air, with the dwellers therein, said, 'Anaximenes was wrong. I am not God!' I asked the heavens, the sun, the moon, and the stars: 'We are not the God whom you seek,' said they. To all the things that stand around the doors of my flesh I said, 'Tell me of my God! Although you are not he, tell me something of him!' With a mighty voice they cried out, 'He made us!' My question was the gaze I turned on them; the answer was their beauty." (*Confessions* 1969, Bk. 10, Ch. 6:9, p.234)

14 "Most blessed (*baruk*) of women be Jael, the wife of Heber the Kenite." Jg. 5:24 (JB).
"This is the blessing with which Moses the man of God blessed the children of Israel before his death. He said . . . 'Blessed (*baruk*) above sons be Asher; let him be the favourite of his brothers.'" Dt. 33:1 and 24
"Uzziah then said to Judith: 'May you be blessed (*baruk*) my daughter by God Most High,' etc." Jth. 13:18 (JB)
Luke's Gospel echoes the proclamations to Jael and Judith: "Elizabeth was filled with the Holy Spirit and she exclaimed with a loud cry, 'Blessed [*eulogeo* from *eu* meaning *good* and *logos* meaning *word*] are you among women and blessed is the fruit of your womb!'" Lk. 1:41f. (JB)

15 "And Melchizedek blessed him and said, 'Blessed (*baruk*) be Abram by God most high, maker of heaven and earth; and blessed (*baruk*) be God most high, who has delivered your enemies into your hand' Gen. 14:18–20 (JB), "
And Jethro said, 'Blessed (*baruk*) be the Lord who has delivered you out of the hands of the Egyptians.'" Ex. 18:10 (JB)

50

THANKSGIVING

"Then the women said to Naomi, 'Blessed (*baruk*) be the Lord who has not left you this day without next of kin.'" Ruth 4:14 (JB)

16   For example: "I thank the Father." Mt. 11:25 (JB); "Anna gave thanks." Lk. 2:38 (JB); "Let us offer the sacrifice of praise to God continually, the fruit of our lips giving thanks to his name." Heb. 13:15 (JB)

17   For example: "There was with the angel a multitude of the heavenly host praising God . . . and the shepherds returned glorifying and praising God." Lk. 2:13, 20 (JB); "Praise the Lord all gentiles and let all the peoples praise him." Rom. 15:11 (JB)

18   For example: "Let your light so shine before men, that they may see your good works and give glory to your father who is in heaven." Mt. 5:16 (JB); "When the crowds saw it, they were afraid and they glorified God." Mt. 9:8 (JB).

19   For example: "And immediately his mouth was opened and his tongue loosed and he spoke blessing God." Lk. 1:64 (JB); "If you bless with the spirit how can anyone with the position of an outsider say the 'Amen!' to your thanksgiving?" 1Cor. 14:16 (JB).

20   Cf. C. Brown, 1978, *Volume III*, p.817. "*Eucharistia*"comes from *eu* meaning "good" and *charis* meaning "gift" or "grace" or "graciousness." "Charis" comes from "chairo" a root word meaning "to be happily at peace."

21   Cf. L. Bouyer 1968, pp.91–135.

22   From "*ex*" and "*stasis*," to stand outside (oneself).

23   "Just as the three disciples in the bright cloud on the mountain experienced a bewildering combination of reverential awe and complete happiness together, so grace, in restoring our lost relationship with God, and thereby putting our ultimate centre outside ourselves, leaves us in a situation which, in practice, often baffles our limited understanding." (A. Squire 1973, p.34)

24   Rom. 8:28. (JB)

25   1Thess. 5:18 (JB) The following prayer found in a concentration camp after World War II captures something of the biblical consciousness permeated by gratitude: "O Lord, remember not only the men of goodwill, but also the men of illwill. But do not remember all the suffering they have inflicted on us, remember the fruits we have gathered thanks to this suffering—our comradeship, our loyalty, our humility, the courage, the generosity, the greatness of heart which has grown out of this—and when they come to judgement, let all the fruits which we have borne be their forgiveness."

4

GOODNESS AND BEAUTY

God saw all he had made, and indeed it was very good. (Gen. 1:31)

The saying is sure. I desire you to insist on these things, so that those who have believed in God may be careful to apply themselves to good deeds; these are excellent and profitable to men. (Titus 3:8)

Let your light so shine before men, that they may see your good works and give glory to your Father who is in heaven. (Mt. 5:16)

THE PICTURE OF DORIAN GRAY

In 1891 Oscar Wilde's short story *The Picture of Dorian Gray* was first published in England. The reaction was both swift and fierce. One paper described it as "a poisonous book, the atmosphere of which is heavy with the mephitic odours of moral and spiritual putrefaction."[1] The story has in fact become one of the better known pieces of modern literature. It is a fable about the beauty of goodness and the ugliness of evil, especially moral evil. The central character, Dorian Gray, is

> wonderfully handsome, with his fiercely curled scarlet lips, his frank blue eyes, his crisp gold hair. There was something in his face that made one trust him at once. All the candour of youth was there, as well as all youth's passionate purity. One felt that he had kept himself unspotted from the world.[2]

He is the subject of a a portrait which is strikingly successful. So successful in fact, that the artist, Basil Hallward, feels he has put his very own soul on view in it and refuses to exhibit the painting. He gives it to Dorian Gray who takes it home and stores it in one of his private rooms.

As the story unfolds, it becomes obvious that Basil has not only expressed his own deepest being in this painting, he has caught the soul and conscience of the handsome young subject and it is very attractive. Attractive that is, until that subject's life begins to disintegrate morally. The painting becomes "a visible symbol of the degradation of sin. Here was an ever-present sign of the ruin men brought upon their souls."[3]

When Dorian becomes aware of this he realizes he has an extraordinary opportunity:

> He felt that the time had really come for making his choice. Or had his choice already been made? Yes, life had decided that for him—life and his own infinite curiosity about life. Eternal youth, infinite passion, pleasures subtle and secret, wild joys and wilder sins—he was to have all these things. The portrait was to bear the burden of his shame, that was all. . . . For there would be a real pleasure in watching it. He would be able to follow his mind into its secret places. This portrait would be to him the most magical of mirrors. As it had revealed to him his own body, so it would reveal to him his own soul. And when winter came upon it, he would still be standing where springs trembles on the verge of summer. When the blood crept from its face, and left behind a pallid mask of chalk with leaden eyes, he would keep the glamour of boyhood. Not one blossom of his loveliness would ever fade. Not one pulse of his life would ever weaken. Like the gods of the Greeks, he would be strong, and fleet, and joyous. What did it matter what happened to the coloured image on the canvas? He would be safe. That was everything.[4]

And so Dorian Gray embarks on a life of promiscuity and unrepented evil. Several people, both men and women, who become intimately involved with with him commit suicide. One other he murders in vengeful spite. Others simply have their reputations ruined through their association with Dorian Gray. His own reputation becomes progressively worse as people find his company more and more repugnant, yet he seems to register nothing of this in his appearance, he remains the handsome and attractive youth of before.

One evening Basil Hallward comes, out of concern for Dorian, to tell him of the terrible things people are saying. He also wants to hear Dorian's own version. Basil is shown the painting that has been hidden in the room upstairs:

> Hallward turned again to the portrait, and gazed at it. "My God! If it is true," he exclaimed, "and this is what you have done with your life, why, you must be worse even than those who talk against you fancy you to be!" He held the light up again to the canvas, and examined it. The surface seemed to be quite undisturbed, and as he had left it. It was from within, apparently, that the foulness and horror had come. Through some strange quickening of inner life the leprosies of sin were

slowly eating the thing away. The rotting of a corpse in a watery grave was not so fearful.[5]

Dorian Gray's life moves ineluctably towards the ugly conclusion intimated by the painting that told of the state of his soul. The hate that he has so wantonly turned on others eventually he turns on himself. Dorian Gray's last desperate act is to try and stab the horrid painting. He stabs himself in the heart instead. The ugliness of his life leaves the painting and manifests itself in him.

THE BEAUTY OF GOODNESS

Goodness attracts us. It has a certain beauty that draws. Evil repels us. It has a certain ugliness that disgusts. If that which is good does in fact repel us, it is because we *perceive* it as evil. If that which is evil attracts us, it is because we *perceive* it as good. As St Augustine writes:

I did not know this at the time but I loved lower beautiful creatures, and I was going down into the very depths. I said to my friends: "Do we love anything except what is beautiful? What then is a beautiful thing? What is beauty? What is it that attracts us and wins us to the things that we love? Unless there were a grace and beauty in them they could in no wise move us."[6]

Later in the same work St Augustine writes what must be one of the most beautiful and insightful passages of all literature:

Too late have I loved you, O Beauty so ancient and so new, too late have I loved you! Behold, you were within me while I was outside; it was there that I sought you, and, a deformed creature, rushed headlong upon these things of beauty which you have made. You were with me but I was not with you.[7]

Goodness—whether it be real or imagined goodness—is compelling. It has a quality that draws and attracts us. And that is precisely the nature of the beautiful. The inner form shines forth and charms and enchants us, more or less.

In the classical Greek tradition, *kalos*, the beautiful, is precisely that *aesthetically pleasing quality* that attends the good—whether it be the practical good or the moral good. William Barclay writes:

We may best of all see the meaning of *kalos*, if we contrast it with *agathos* which is the common Greek word for *good*. *Agathos* is that which is practically and morally good; *kalos* is not only that which is

55

practically and morally good, but that which is also aesthetically good, which is lovely and pleasing to the eye. . . . When a thing or person is *agathos*, it or he is good in the moral and practical sense of the term, and in the result of its or his activity; but *kalos* adds to the idea of goodness the idea of beauty, of loveliness, of graciousness, of winsomeness. *Agathos* appeals to the moral sense; but *kalos* appeals also to the eye.[8]

Genuine virtue has a gracious quality about it. Truly virtuous people are attractive people. Thus when that great desert ascetic of the 4th century, Anthony, emerged from the awful rigors of his years of fasting, people flocked to him. They sought him out because he had a certain radiance about him, as much gentle as wise.

Recall the words of Jesus: "And when you fast, do not look dismal, like the hypocrites, for they disfigure their faces that their fasting may be seen by men. Truly, I say to you, they have received their reward."[9] Or in another place: "My yoke is easy, and my burden is light."[10] There is a marked sense of ease about the moral teaching of Jesus. To be moral in the Christian sense is to submit and receive grace. The essence of Christian morality is found in the primacy of grace—God's self-giving.

Pseudo "virtue" fails to appreciate the primacy of gift. It starts with duty and what *we* must do. A sign of pseudo virtue is its lack of graciousness. It is always forced. Pseudo virtue lacks gentleness, and is generally tightly controlled. The body often records it with tight muscles. Because all genuine virtue is grace, pure gift, it is typically accompanied by a sense of freedom. When we catch ourselves the recipients of virtue— "being virtuous"—we ought to be surprised. A most appropriate reaction to discovering oneself being blessed in this way is gratitude. An inappropriate reaction and a tell tale sign of some work to do is the feeling of satisfaction when we find virtue coming into the world via us. Barclay goes on to write:

> Clearly it is not enough that the Christian life should be good; it must also be attractive. A grim and unlovely goodness is certainly goodness, but it is not "Christian" goodness; for Christian goodness must have a certain loveliness on it. Real Christianity must always attract and never repel. There is such a thing as a hard, austere, unlovely and unlovable goodness, but such a goodness falls far short of the Christian standard. In all his efforts to be good, in all his strivings towards moral holiness, the Christian must never forget the "beauty of holiness."[11]

THE CONCEPT OF GOODNESS IN THE OLD TESTAMENT

In the OT the word for *good* is *tob* and it is frequently situated in contrast to *evil—wara*. Thus: "to know good and evil";[12] "to distinguish between good and evil";[13] "to refuse the evil and choose the good";[14] "to depart from evil and do good";[15] "seek good and not evil";[16] "to hate evil and love good."[17]

All that is "good" comes from the Lord of the Exodus. Words such as *"hesed," "rahamim"* and *"emet"* all in different ways point to the gracious "goodness" of the Lord manifest in the Covenant. It is these qualities that separate the God of Israel from the other gods and keep drawing the people back to the Covenant relationship.[18]

An idea of the good freed from the concept of a personal God is inconceivable. The good is always a gift from God and as such is ultimately outside our control, beyond our strength.[19] It is presupposed throughout that God is the one who is good and not just "the good." This realization is further developed within the OT in the course of a deepening of the relationship of the people and of individuals to God.[20]

The Hebrew *"tob"* is almost always translated in the Septuagint by *"to agathon"* "and thus approaches the Greco-Hellenistic outlook. It only rarely employs the nearly synonymous *kalos* (e.g. Gen. 1:18)."[21]

Apart from the saving event of Exodus and its Covenant, God's goodness is manifest in his giving of the Law,[22] His work of creation,[23] His word,[24] His spirit,[25] and even when appearances seem to say the opposite.[26] In a word, it is the remembrance of the Covenant that gives the people an unshakable conviction of the goodness of God that is everlasting. Job is a classic example of the refusal to deny the goodness of God, even amidst the most horrific evidence of evil.[27]

THE CONCEPT OF GOOD IN THE NEW TESTAMENT

Jesus, loyal son of the Covenant and its mindset, reflects the deeply ingrained perception that God alone is good and all goodness is in some way a participation in his goodness.[28] In the NT, the words most frequently used to render *"good"* are *"agathos," "chrestos"* and *"kalos"*. It is the last of these, *"kalos,"* which William Barclay is considering in depth when he makes the comment to which we referred earlier in this reflection. Only by understanding this word within the total biblical context can we maintain its authentic Christian implications. Brown notes:

The meaning which the Greeks gave to "*kalos*," which became decisive for Christian antiquity and via Christendom for the development of thought throughout the western world, scarcely penetrated the world of the OT or the NT. . . . "*kalos*" appears most frequently beside "*agathos*" and "*chrestos*" as a translation of "*tob*" (in the Septuagint). It means good, not so much in the sense of an ethical evaluation, as in that of pleasant, enjoyable, beneficial. "*Kalos*," as opposed to "*agathos*," is what is pleasing to Yahweh, what he likes or what gives him joy, whereas "*agathos*" suggests more the application of an ethical standard. But it is impossible to draw any clear-cut lines of demarcation for the basic meaning of the Hebrew "*tob*" for it contains both aspects. It is striking that there is no room in the OT for the Greek ideal of beauty as a motive for living and for education. Everything is directed towards the will of God which is expressed in the Law. Any ideal of self-perfection is thus excluded.[29]

Throughout the NT "*kalos*"is used almost as frequently as "*agathos*"—the former 99 times, the latter 104 times. We find "*kalos*" and its cognates used in the following instances: John the Baptist demands "good fruit" of those who wish to enter the kingdom;[30] the parables speak of "good seed,"[31] "good ground";[32] "the good and useful fish,"[33] "the good salt,"[34] "the good measure generously given";[35] Jesus calls people to "good works";[36] Jesus is "the good shepherd";[37] Jesus does "many good works";[38] the temple is "adorned with noble (i.e. "good") stones";[39] the name of Christ is "good";[40] the word of God is "good."[41] "The preference for "kalos" in the Pastorals (1 and 2 Timothy and Titus) is striking."[42]

PRACTICAL INSIGHTS ARISING

Some practical insights for Christian life formation emerge from the foregoing. In the first place "the Christian teaching must be 'kalos'" (1Tim. 4:6).[43] The goodness and beauty of the Christ event ought to shine through our words and actions. The preacher and teacher of the Good News ought to be transparent therefore. The self-centered, insecure strivings of the ego are opaque, they block the flow of the Mystery. They are, compared with the freeing potential of that Mystery, decidedly unlovely—even if very attractive to some. There is of course always the possibility that the hearers may find the message "too hard"—as they did sometimes with Christ—and reject it as unlovely, unattractive, even evil. We ought not be too quick to jump to this conclusion however.[44]

In the second place emphasizing the goodness/beauty of the Good News does not imply a pseudo joy, a superficial charm or a compromising of the "hard sayings" of Jesus. It is, rather, to begin to sense something of the truth that his "yoke is easy, (his) burden is light."[45] When we have tasted the real thing all else will tend to be less attractive, no matter what it costs to continue tasting the real thing.[46]

The delight that characterizes the Christian is beyond mere emotional titillation. It is the sense that accompanies the conviction that "Christ has died, Christ is risen and Christ will come again." This good and beautiful truth, when it takes hold of our consciousness, enables us to live the tragedy of human existence and walk with others in that tragedy without succumbing to despair, cynicism or even willful resignation. It means that a consciousness captured by the Mystery of the New Covenant always gives the last word to goodness and beauty, not evil and ugliness. Like our ancestor Job we refuse to curse God even amidst circumstances most favorable to that curse. And like Jesus on the cross we can cry in anguish "My God, my God, why have you forsaken me!" without yielding to the forces of darkness.[47]

In the third place a besetting sin of conscientiously religious people is despondency and discouragement. In the tales of the Hasidim we read:

> Guard yourself from despondency above all, for it is worse and more harmful than sin. When the Evil Urge wakens desires in man, he is not concerned with plunging him into sin, but with plunging him into despondency by way of sin.[48]

Francis de Sales picks up the same theme in the beginning of his *Introduction to the Devout Life* when he speaks of the dangers of allowing discouragement to take over. Julian of Norwich is another great proponent of the confidence that overcomes such discouragement.[49] Despondency and discouragement may be a sign that the ego is upset over its inability to measure up to an idealized image. Genuine shame and guilt may emerge quite healthily in those who know they have chosen evil rather than good, yet, if the focus remains essentially with God who has graciously bound himself to us by Covenant, that shame and guilt bring us quickly into an experience of his mercy and compassion which is faithful from generation to generation.

In the fourth place another besetting sin of the conscientiously religious person is dualism. Matter—which is supposed to be evil—is separated from spirit—which is supposed to be good. This is contrary to the biblical revelation yet it is amazingly frequent in the Christian tradition. Louis Bouyer writes:

> The chief deviation to which the ascetic ideal of the first centuries was sometimes reduced in popular literature was an insistence on continence so fervent that it came rather to neglect its motivations. Then, under the influence of the pessimistic dualism of the period, marriage came to be condemned along with the whole of life in the flesh. This is what is called "encratism."[50]

In our own recent tradition the Jansenism of seventeenth century France, and the earlier Calvinism of the Reformers, has been influential. Thus we have found it difficult to be convinced of the loveliness and goodness of the human body and its sensual delights, or, in some extremes, anything pleasurable. It is surely a terrible travesty of the Good News to imply that the Christ Event does not also redeem the pleasurable possibilities in our human existence.[51]

In the fifth place the "willpower Christianity" so characteristic of the recent centuries also tends to foster a joyless Christianity. It focuses too much attention on the human will and the person's obligations to "measure up." It is really another form of the Pelagianism against which Augustine fought so hard in the fourth and fifth centuries. When we lose that primary focus on the Mystery of saving love we also tend to lose our sense of being graciously loved into freedom. This leaves us, psychologically, carrying a terrible burden. No matter how much we talk about the God of love and the Good News, they remain an abstraction because deep in our guts we feel awfully responsible for our salvation. There is little goodness or beauty in behavior springing from this motivation.

PRACTICAL SUGGESTIONS

(a) This week, notice the world of nature around you—trees, sun, clouds, wind, flowers, other people caught up in the mystery of life. Stop and stare. Listen. Receive. Let yourself be overtaken by the mystery of it all.

(b) Recall someone you would say was a particularly good person. Why do you say they are "good"? What qualities does this "goodness" radiate? What sort of reaction does it evoke in you? What is happening in you?

(c) Conscience is a deep gut sense-ability, an ability to sense good and evil, right and wrong. It involves the whole person. It is the kind of "knowing" about which Jesus speaks when he talks of "knowing the Father" and he and the disciples "knowing" each other. It is the ability to detect evil posing as good, the allurement and pseudo beauty of the demonic. A mature person fosters this "deep gut sense" by repeatedly aligning him or herself with the good—he or she "knows" deep in his or her being what the good and the true is like. Reflect on your own experience of a developing conscience.

Notes
1   Cited in the Introduction to *Oscar Wilde*, Octopus Books, 1983, p.11. Perhaps a comment Wilde had made in the Preface to *The Picture of Dorian Gray* was borne out by some of the reviews: "The highest, as the lowest form of criticism is a mode of autobiography" (*The Collected Works of Oscar Wilde*, 1970, p. 17). Or again in the story itself, Lord Henry Wotton observes: "None of us can stand other people having the same faults as ourselves." (p.22)
2   Op. cit., p.27.
3   Op. cit., p.81.
4   Op. cit., p.87f.
5   Op. cit., p.122.
6   *Confessions* 1969, Book 4, Chapter 13, p.106. Aristotle seems to be pointing to the same thing when he argues that, above all, we wish the good for ourselves (cf. *Nichomachean Ethics*, 9, 4, 1166a). St Thomas Aquinas says something similar: "The human person desires happiness naturally and by necessity." (S.T. I, 94, 1)
7   Op. cit., Book X, Chapter 27, p.254.
8   W. Barclay 1980, p.154.
9   Mt. 6:16.
10   Mt. 11:30.
11   W. Barclay, op. cit., 156f.
12   Gen. 2:9–17; 3:5–22; Dt. 1:39.
13   2Sam. 19:36; 1Kg. 3:9; Dt. 1:16.
14   Is. 7:15f.
15   Ps. 34:14; 37:27.
16   Amos 5:14.
17   Amos 5:15; Mic. 3:2.
18   The Psalms are redolent with this acknowledgment of the goodness and uniqueness of God compared with other gods: "Those who choose another god multiply their sorrows; their libations of blood I will not pour out or take their names upon my lips." Ps. 16:4; "Blessed is the man who makes the LORD his trust, who does not turn to the proud, to those who go astray after false gods!" Ps. 40:4; "He only is my rock and my salvation, my fortress; I shall not be greatly moved." Ps. 62:2; "Thy way, O God, is holy. What god is great like our God?" Ps. 77:13.
19   Cf. Gen. 3:5.
20   For example: Pss. 34:10; 84:11; 23:6. Cf. C. Brown, op. cit., Volume 2, p.99.
21   Ibid.
22   Cf. Dt. 30:15; Prov. 28:10.
23   Cf. Gen. 1:18; *tob* here also implies beauty.
24   Cf. Is. 39:8.

25 Ps. 143:10.
26 Cf. Gen. 50:20.
27 The Jewish scholar Arthur Hertzberg offers a contemporary Jewish perspective: "A number of my friends who were firmly Orthodox before 1933, became fierce atheists. I have not joined them because I keep reading the Book of Job. Every conceivable woe happens to this righteous man, Job. He rejects all the explanations that his solicitous friends try to offer him. Ultimately he summons God to give him an answer. Replying out of the whirlwind, God offers Job no explanation, but He does not disclaim responsibility. 'Where were you,' God asks Job, 'when I founded the world?' His powers are indeed unlimited, and he is never absent from the world, either by choice or because he is in eclipse. God simply asserts that there is meaning to the world, and even to Job's suffering, but it is beyond man's understanding. And yet, even as I read these verses over and over again, I keep asking the question: what about Job's children? Job survived the tragedy of their death, but could he ever forgive God? Why God was silent from 1939 to 1945 will forever be a mystery. The disbeliever will insist that this silence proves God's irrelevance or his non-existence; the believer will hold on to the faith that the world adds up, but only in the mind of God." (1992, p.244). (Note: Hertzberg, who lived in the United States during the World War II, lost his grandfather and "all of my mother's brothers and sisters and their children" in the holocaust; cf. op. cit., p.243.)
28 Cf. Mk. 10:17f.; Lk. 18:18f.; Mt. 19:17.
29 C. Brown, op. cit., 103.
30 Mt. 3:10. Cf. also Lk. 3:9; Mt. 7:17–19; 12:33; Lk. 6:43.
31 Cf. Mt. 13:24.
32 Cf. Mt. 13:23.
33 Cf. Mt. 13:48.
34 Cf. Mk. 9:50.
35 Cf. Lk. 6:38.
36 Cf. Mt. 5:16.
37 Cf. Jn. 10:11.
38 Cf. Jn. 10:31.
39 Cf. Lk. 21:5.
40 Cf. Jm. 2:7.
41 Cf. Heb. 5:14.
42 C. Brown, op. cit., p.104. The word appears 24 times in these Letters. Cf. 1 Tim. 5:10: "a widow . . . must be well-attested for her good deeds"; 6:18: "the rich in this world . . . are to do good, to be rich in good deeds, liberal and generous"; Tit. 2:7: "show yourself in all respects a model of good deeds"; 1 Tim. 1:8: "we know that the law is good if anyone uses it lawfully"; 4:4: "for everything created by God is good."
43 W. Barclay, op. cit., p.158.
44 Cf. "The Pastoral Constitution on the Church in the Modern World," n. 19. There the Second Vatican Council reminds us that "believers themselves frequently bear some responsibility" for the irreligion and atheism in our world. For a very good discussion of St Paul's description of the preacher, see J. Murphy-O'Connor 1963. Paul makes it very clear that the preacher is a servant of the Mystery that has taken hold of him or her.
45 Cf. Mt. 11:30.
46 "Indeed I count everything as loss because of the surpassing worth of knowing Christ Jesus my Lord. For his sake I have suffered the loss of all things, and count them as refuse, in order that I may gain Christ . . . ." (Phil. 3:8); "Finally, brethren, whatever is true, whatever is honorable, whatever is just, whatever is pure, whatever is lovely, whatever is gracious, if there is any excellence, if there is anything worthy of praise, think about these things" (Phil. 4:8).

47 Cf. M. D. Molinie 1977.
48 M. Buber 1948, p.315.
49 See also *Fénelon's Spiritual Letters*, pp.41, 51, 68 and 73f. The English Dominican Gerald Vann writes: "The desert was the appropriate place for the first temptation: in an arid, unpeopled wilderness it is easy to fall into melancholy, to feel a desolation and affliction of spirit, to feel the lack of human companionship, human sympathy or perhaps admiration. And in such conditions it is easy to fall victim to sensual temptations of some kind, for nature then inclines us to look for pleasures by way of compensation for the feelings of sadness and desolation." 1966, p.84.
50 L. Bouyer n.d., p.189.
51 Perhaps this same dualism has been influential in the disrespect shown for the environment over the past century or so?

5
MISSING THE MARK

So when the woman saw that the tree was good for food, and that it was a delight to the eyes, and that the tree was to be desired to make one wise, she took of its fruit and ate; and she also gave some to her husband, and he ate. (Gen 3:6)

To set the mind on the flesh is death, but to set the mind on the Spirit is life and peace. (Rom. 8:6)

And as he sat at table in the house, behold, many tax collectors and sinners came and sat down with Jesus and his disciples. (Mt. 9:10)

MAREI THE PEASANT

In *The Diary of a Writer*, Fyodor Dostoievsky records an incident from childhood that was to stay with him and give him light and encouragement in his darkest days.[1] There was a little wood called Brykovo near Darovoe where his family lived. The nine-year-old Dostoievsky was forbidden to play in the wood for fear of wolves and snakes. One day, however, he was playing there when he thought he heard someone call out "Wolf!" He ran screaming from the wood and found the family's serf, Marei, working in the field nearby. Later Dostoievsky was to describe the event as follows:

It was our peasant Marei . . . a man in his fifties, tall and strong, with a thick red beard streaked with grey. I knew him though I had never spoken to him. Hearing my screams, he had stopped his mare, and when I reached him and grasped his sleeve with one hand and the plough with the other, he realised my terror. "Wolf!" I repeated panting. He raised his head and looked around him. For a moment he almost believed me. "Where is the wolf?" "Someone shouted—they shouted wolf!" I stammered. "Come on, there's no wolf, you dreamed it. What would a wolf be doing here?" he murmured, to reassure me. But I clutched his blouse and trembled all the more, and I suppose I must have turned still paler. "Well, well, you really are frightened," he said, nodding his head, "come now, little one, it's all over. See how brave he is!" He put out a hand and patted my cheek. "Come on, it's all finished. God bless you. Cross yourself now." But I didn't cross myself. The corner of my lips were twitching. He noticed it and put his thick black-nailed finger, stained with earth, on my nervous lips. . .

And then, twenty years later, in Siberia, I remembered this meeting in its minutest details. I saw once more the tender, motherly smile of the poor peasant, our serf. I remembered him crossing himself and nodding: "You really are frightened, little one!" And especially the big earth-stained finger with which he had grazed my lips softly, almost shyly. And suddenly I jumped up from my straw-bed and, glancing around, I felt that I could see these poor wretches in a quite different light, and by a sudden magic, all hatred and anger vanished from my heart.[2]

This little vignette from the life and thought of Dostoievsky gives us some insight into a theme that was to become like a leitmotif in his writings: the distinction between good and evil. One commentator notes of Dostoievksy's reflections arising out of his prison years:

Even in these murderers and miscreants, Dostoievsky found a spark of humanity and a glimmer of the divine. For them too, the distinction between good and evil was the fundamental human category. And out of this observation sprang his belief that the people in their besmirched lowliness hid a promise of mercy and a dream of Christ.[3]

In *Crime and Punishment*, Dostoievsky takes up the theme of good and evil with a profundity seldom equalled. Most particularly he is concerned to explore the the nature and origins of evil. The main character, a young student by the name of Rodion Romanovitch Raskolnikov, known as Rodya, commits a double murder as an experiment to see if he is able to break free of society's constraints and fabricate his own sense of good and evil. The following discussion between Rodya, Razumihin, Rodya's devoted friend and fiancé to Rodya's sister Dounia, and Porfiry, the brilliant detective who is more interested in helping the murderer than prosecuting him, raises the question as to the origin of evil actions:

"Only fancy, Rodya, what we got on to yesterday. Whether there is such a thing as crime. I told you that we talked our heads off."
"What is there strange? It's an everyday social question," Raskolnikov answered casually.
"The question wasn't put quite like that," observed Porfiry.
"Not quite, that's true," Razumihin agreed at once, getting warm and hurried as usual. "Listen, Rodion, tell us your opinion, I want to hear it. I was fighting tooth and nail with them and wanted you to help me. I told them you were coming . . . It began with the socialist doctrine.

You know their doctrine; crime is a protest against the abnormality of the social organization and nothing more, and nothing more; no other causes admitted!. . ."

"You are wrong there," cried Porfiry Petrovitch; he was noticeably animated and kept laughing as he looked at Razumihin which made him more excited than ever.

"Nothing is admitted," Razumihin interrupted with heat.

"I am not wrong. I'll show you their pamphlets. Everything with them is 'the influence of environment,' and nothing else. Their favourite phrase! From which it follows that, if society is normally organized, all crime will become righteous in one instant. Human nature is not taken into account, it is excluded, it's not supposed to exist! They don`t recognise that humanity, developing by a historical living process, will become at last a normal society, but they believe that a social system that has come out of some mathematical brain is going to organize all humanity at once and make it just and sinless in an instant, quicker than any living process! That's why they instinctively dislike history, 'nothing but ugliness and stupidity in it,' and they explain it all as stupidity! That's why they so dislike the *living* process of life; they don't want a *living soul*! The living soul demands life, the soul won't obey the rules of mechanics, the soul is an object of suspicion, the soul is retrograde! But what they want though it smells of death and can be made of india-rubber, at least is not alive, has no will, is servile and won't revolt! And it comes in the end to their reducing everything to the building of walls and the planning of rooms and passages in a phalanstery! The phalanstery is ready, indeed, but your human nature is not ready for the phalanstery!—it wants life, it hasn't completed its vital process, it's too soon for the graveyard! You can't skip over nature by logic. Logic presupposes three possibilities, but there are millions! Cut away a million, and reduce it all to the question of comfort! That's the easiest solution of the problem! It's seductively clear and you mustn't think about it. That's the great thing, you mustn't think! The whole secret of life in two pages of print!"

"Now he is off, beating the drum! Catch hold of him, do!" laughed Porfiry. "Can you imagine," he turned to Raskolnikov, "six people holding forth like that last night, in one room, with punch as a preliminary! No, brother, you are wrong, environment accounts for a great deal in crime; I can assure you of that."

"Oh, I know it does, but just tell me: a man of forty violates a child of ten; was it environment drove him to it?"

"Well, strictly speaking, it did," Porfiry observed with noteworthy gravity; "a crime of that nature may be very well ascribed to the influence of environment."

Razumihin was almost in a frenzy. "Oh, if you like," he roared. "I'll prove to you that your white eyelashes may very well be ascribed to the Church of Ivan the Great's being two hundred and fifty feet high, and I will prove it clearly, exactly, progressively, and even with a Liberal tendency! I undertake to! Will you bet on it?"[4]

SIN IN THE BIBLE

In the OT there is a clear recognition of sin but no clear or systematic theology of sin developed. Like Dostoievsky it struggles to understand and account for the evil that is so evident in human behavior. Bernhard Anderson writes of the primeval history of Genesis 1–11:

> This is a true story, not because it represents accurate ancient history, but because it portrays realistically the world in which we live: a world in which human beings are called to responsibility and in which their actions have inescapable consequences. In a profound sense we are 'in Adam,' the type who represents humanity in its sin and failure.[5]

In the Septuagint two words, "*hamartia*" and "*adikia*," represent between them almost the whole range of Hebrew words for guilt and sin.[6] The root word from which *hamartia* is drawn means literally *to miss, miss the mark, lose, not share in something, be mistaken.*[7] Thus, in the OT context the notion of sin implies some kind of misplaced relationship—in a word, missing the point of the Covenant. Adam's misdirection and misplacement of his inherent longings as a person—and particularly as a person created and elected by God—is an archetype of *hamartia*, sin. Later the building of the tower of Babel[8] expresses the same misplacement of human longings and energies, with the particular consequence that human beings henceforward will not be able to communicate easily with each other, their words turn to "babble." Sin sets human existence in a direction away from God, from "what is" towards "what is not," from "reality" towards "illusion."[9]

In the NT "all the other concepts and synonyms (for sin) are overshadowed by *hamartia* and are to be understood in the light of this concept."[10] The Gospel of John and the Letters of Paul offer the deepest development of the Christian understanding of sin. The word *hamartia* occurs 173 times in the NT, and 64 of those instances are to be found in

Paul. The word *hamartia* is always used in the NT of human sin which is ultimately directed against God.[11] In the synoptic Gospels it is found almost exclusively in the context of the forgiveness of sins, though here the connotation is generally that the Law has been broken. In the Sermon on the Mount, however, Jesus goes beyond the Jewish concept of The Law as the yardstick and sets his person and teaching as a new standard.[12]

It is to "sinners"—not the righteous—that Jesus comes.[13] Thus He is called "the friend of sinners."[14] The irony is that all are "sinners." And perhaps the ultimate sin, the ultimate missing of the mark, is that someone should believe he or she is not in need of the freedom Jesus offers.[15] Jesus is "the way, the truth and the life."[16] He provides "the light"[17] by which all peoples—bound as we are by the propensity to constantly miss the point of life—can see. If we make our home in his word we will learn the truth and the truth will set us free.[18]

For John, Jesus is the way, not a set of regulations and dogmas. "I am the way." The call to follow is not a call to willfully pursue a preset ethical standard. It is rather a call to allow God to make a home in us.[19] Jesus does not just point—he provides the very Energy to go where he points.

St Paul's understanding of sin is found largely in Romans, Chapters 1–8. For Paul, human existence disconnected from God is a dark world, a world of disordered passion and misdirected endeavor. He commonly uses the word "*sarx*"—unfortunately translated in English by the misleading word "flesh"—to describe that spiritless world. *Sarx* is contrasted with "*pneuma*"—again lamely translated by the English word "spirit"—which is the world of light, the world in which human energies and longings are caught up in the liberating Mystery revealed in Christ. Similar to the Johannine mysticism where the emphasis is on the indwelling Trinity, the Pauline approach to the same issue of co-operating with grace and living the redemptive life emphasizes the mystery of Christ that lives in us and takes over.[20]

PRACTICAL INSIGHTS ARISING

Some practical insights for Christian life formation emerge from the foregoing. In the first place all human life formation is fallen or flawed life formation. That is, we are constantly subject to the reality of missing the mark, misdirecting our energies and talents, choosing unwisely, misplacing our efforts. We need to be shown the way, to be constantly brought back to the way. This is one of the three interdependent foundations of

Christian spirituality. The other two are that we are made in the image and likeness of God, and that we are redeemed in Christ. Miss one of these foundations or overemphasize it and you finish with a distorted picture of Christian life formation.

We also need to respond and work at this task of acknowledging when and where we have missed the way and submit again and again to the healing and guiding Spirit of Christ. The Christian life is an ongoing process in which we facilitate the emergence of the Christ form given in its own unique way to each baptized person. We do that humbly, sometimes painfully, always with thanksgiving for the mercy and goodness of God. St Augustine's observation is apt: "Better to stumble along the way than race by the way."[21]

In the second place this missing of the mark that permeates human existence points to the tragic dimension of our attempted relationships. Simone Weil writes: "God and humanity are like two lovers who have missed their rendezvous."[22] Despite our best efforts to link up with God and unite our lives with him absolutely, we always fall short. That's the way it is! And that's also the way it is with those we attempt to love here and now. We are constantly made aware of how infrequently we ever actually "rendezvous" with others. There is a part of each of us that can never be reached by another, we must be there alone. And even in that relationship with the self we constantly miss out, choosing the illusory self over the real self time and again. Perhaps it is also why organizing human societies—politics in other words—is the "the art of the possible," where the better can be the enemy of the good. Simone Weil, in the text already cited above, goes on to say:

> Each is there before the time, but each is at a different place, and they wait, and wait, and wait. He stands motionless, nailed to the spot for the whole of time. She is distraught and impatient. But alas for her if she gets tired and goes away. . . . The crucifixion of Christ is the image of the fixity of God.[23]

In the third place, in this context we are reminded of the relativity of any historical moment or cultural milieu. In an era such as ours, with so many possibilities opening up before us and so much awareness of the inadequacies of the past, we may forget that we too will miss the mark just as surely as any previous generation. What will history say of us in the year 3000? There is wisdom and compassion in the words of Jean Danielou:

I have no liking for Christians who will not touch the facts of human existence for fear of soiling their hands. The Christians who struggle to make Christianity effective in the world, even at the cost of painful blows, those I admire. I love that Church which plunges into the thickets of human history and is not afraid of compromising itself by getting mixed up with men's affairs, with their political conflicts and their cultural disputes. I love that Church because it loves men and therefore goes out to look for them wherever they are. And I love best of all that Church which is mudsplashed from history because it has played its part in history, that Church of the poor which is denounced for its weaknesses by pharisees whose hands are clean but who can point to no single person they have saved.[24]

In the fourth place, in the light of all the foregoing it is well for each of us to foster a gentle and forgiving self-presence. We will lurch through life, constantly misplacing our energies, constantly missing the point—hopefully less and less so as we grow in age and wisdom. Such lurching should make us compassionate towards others and remind us of the wonderful mercy of God. "God so loved the world He sent His only Son" to seek us out and lead us home.[25] My missing the mark is not the final point. To miss that truth might perhaps be the greatest tragedy of all. The final point is God's mercy. My confidence and joy as a Christian does not spring from my personal "successes" but from my conviction that my Redeemer lives![26]

In the fifth place, in the course of our lives those unmistakable echoes of death that reach us from time to time tend to clarify our sight, purging us of attachments that do not really matter and allowing us to see and direct our attention to what really matters.[27] In the face of death, it seems, human beings are more likely to direct their attentions appropriately. It is interesting to note the wisdom of little children who are terminally ill. Perhaps the knowledge of impending death enables us to shed so much of the baggage in a brief span of days that otherwise would take many years, and even then may not happen.

PRACTICAL SUGGESTIONS

(a) In the coming week pay close attention to moments of frustration, impatience and intolerance—with yourself and other people, events and things. Reflect on these experiences in the light of God's gracious mercy: "My yoke is easy, my burden is light." Ask the open questions: What is happening here? What are you feeling? What is this revealing about your attitudes to yourself, other people, events and things? (b) Consider your education in Christian life formation. Have those three foundations been kept in creative tension: that we are made in the image and likeness of God, fallen, and redeemed in Christ? How do you keep that creative tension?

(c) Is it possible for you to have a good self-image without also having a clear sighted sense of your potential for evil?

Notes

1 In 1846 the the twenty-five-year-old Dostoievsky met Petrachevksy, a man from the Foreign Office, who gathered a small group of young liberal thinkers for discussions in his house. They often enough criticized the regime and the current situation of many of the people. The police introduced a spy into the group and thirty-three of them—including Dostoievsky—were arrested in April of 1849. Later, during ten weeks of solitary confinement, Dostoievsky learned that his older brother Michel and younger brother Andre, arrested by mistake at the same time, had been released. After five months of hearings the commission of investigation appointed by the Tsar admitted his innocence. However, at the request of the Minister for the Interior, they agreed to impose a punishment. Thus, Dostoievksy and several of the others were sentenced to death, with a suggestion being made to the Emperor that they should be reprieved at the same time and given hard labor instead. Three days before Christmas in 1849, Dostoievsky and his friends were led out to be shot. There was an execution parade, a reading of the death sentence and a sermon by a priest. Only at the last moment of this brutal comedy, with the executioners taking aim at the first three condemned men, was the order given to stop. On Christmas Eve he and the others were shipped off to Siberia with shackles on their arms and ten pound weights attached to their ankles. Dostoievsky served four years of hard labor there.

2 Cited by Gilbert Sigaux, "A Portrait of Dostoievsky," a foreword to *Crime and Punishment*, J. M. Dent & Sons, (date unknown), pp.x–xi.

3 Geir Kjetsaa 1989, p.107. Alexander Solzhenitsyn's experience is somewhat similar to that of Dostoievsky: "It was granted to me to carry away from my prison years on my bent back, which nearly broke beneath its load, this essential experience: *how* a human being becomes evil and *how* good. In the intoxication of youthful successes I had felt myself to be infallible, and I was therefore cruel. In the surfeit of power I was a murderer, and an oppressor. In my most evil moments I was convinced that I was doing good, and I was well supplied with systematic arguments. And it was only when I lay there on rotting prison straw that I sensed within myself the first stirrings of good. Gradually it was disclosed to me that the line separating good and evil passes not through states, nor between classes, nor between political parties either—but right through every human heart . . . Since then I have come to understand the truth of all the religions of the world: they struggle with the *evil inside a human being* (inside every human being). It is impossible to expel evil from the world in its entirety but it is possible to constrict it within each person. And since that time I have come to understand the falsehood of all revolutions in history: They destroy only *those carriers* of evil contemporary with them (and also fail, out of haste, to discriminate the carriers of good as well). And they then take to themselves as their heritage the actual evil itself, magnified still more." Alexander Solzhenitsyn, 1975, pp.615–16).

4 Dostoievski 1982, Part III, Chapter V, pp. 250–2.
5 B. Anderson 1979, 73. Cf. also Eugene Maly 1979, 40–8.
6 Cf. C. Brown, 1979, Volume 3, p.577.
7 Ibid.
8 Cf. Gen. 11.
9 Jesuit theologian Robert Gleason has described sin as an existential leap in the direction of nowhere.
10 C. Brown, op. cit., p.579.
11 Cf. Ibid.
12 Cf. for example, Mt. 7:21.
13 Cf. Mt. 9:13.
14 Mt. 9:10. Cf. also Lk. 7:36ff., 15:1ff, 18:9ff, 19:1ff.
15 Cf. The parable of the Pharisee and the Publican, Lk. 18:10ff.
16 Jn. 14:6.
17 Jn. 1:4ff.
18 Cf. Jn. 8:32.
19 Cf. Jn. 14:23.
20 Cf. Gal. 2:20; Rom. 6:3; Phil. 3:13; Col. 1:26.
21 Cf. Adrian Van Kaam's discussion of "existential transferrence" in *Religion and Personality* (revised edition 1980). See also P. Brown 1969, especially Chapter 15.
22 Simone Weil, "The Things of the World" in G. Panichas 1977, p.424.
23 Ibid.
24 J. Danielou, 1967, p.55.
25 Cf. Jn. 3:16.
26 Cf. A. Van Kaam 1980, 14–15.
27 "So teach us to number our days that we may get a heart of wisdom." Ps. 90:12

6

IMAGES OF GOD— PRELIMINARY EXPLORATIONS

Yahweh, Yahweh, a God of tenderness and compassion, slow to anger, rich in kindness and faithfulness (Ex. 34:6)

From the throne where you sit as righteous judge. (Ps. 9:4)

It was the third hour when they crucified him. The inscription giving the charge against him read: "The King of the Jews". And they crucified two robbers with him, one on his right and one on his left. (Mk. 15:26f.)

GOD IN THE WHITE FOLKS' BIBLE

There is an unnerving, earthy honesty in the "letters" that form the substance of Alice Walker's novel, *The Color Purple*. Celie, the main character, normally writes to God and speaks of what has been happening in her life. She has grown a little annoyed and disillusioned with God so she writes to her sister Nettie who has gone to Africa with some white missionaries. In one of those letters—the very epitome of earthy honesty—Celie records her conversation with the vivacious and mischievous Shug.

When Shug asks Celie to tell her who God is for her, Celie replies: "he big and old and tall and graybearded and white." "This old white man," says Shug, is the same God she used to see in her imagination when she prayed. "That's the one that's in the white folks' white bible."

It takes little prompting from Shug for Celie to see the connection between this image of God and the situation of oppression in which she lives: "I know white people never listen to coloured."

Shug then goes on to describe her own reconstructed image of God. It makes Celie think. The conversation finishes with Celie musing:

"Well, us talk and talk bout God, but I'm still adrift. Trying to chase that ole white man out of my head. I been so busy thinking bout him I never truly notice nothing God make. Not a blade of corn (how it do that?) not the color purple (where it come from?). Not the little wildflowers. Nothing."[1]

OUR IMAGES AND PERCEPTIONS

Perhaps one of the most deceptive things about formalized religious language is its implication or presupposition that we know what/who we are talking about when we say God, or that two people are talking about the same thing when they talk about God. The Bible, in fact, gives us no clear single definition of God. It gives some very definite pointers—through historical events, myths, adjectives, images, symbols, names and so on—which we are left to ponder in our own communal and individual ways. We leave our encounters with the sacred text pointed in a certain direction, which may be more or less creative and formative or more or less destructive and deformative, depending on what we have been willing and or able to let happen in that encounter.

In this chapter we will look more particularly at some of the factors involved in us as *perceiving and imagining subjects*. In the following chapter we will try to explore the territory beyond our perceptions and images and look more particularly at some of the factors involved in *"the object" of our perceptions and imaginings*. Throughout, we will use the term "images" in the broadest sense as meaning mental constructs. It thus connotes ideas as well as phantasms. To emphasize this broad use, the word images will normally be used with the word perceptions. Also, for the time being, we will be working on the assumption that when the word "God" is used, it points—no matter how vaguely—to the infinite, the ultimate, Reality beyond reality, the ground of all that is. There is no question of proving the existence of such a dimension—it is assumed.[2]

In the Introduction we stressed the importance of consciousness. Consciousness plays a key role in the formulation of what we call reality. The human world of everyday living is co-constituted—persons interact with people, events and things, and the result is what we call reality. This is not to say that reality is simply subjective. It is to say that no person or group of persons ever perceives and speaks of "what is" in a purely true and utterly objective way. Nobody has the whole picture, the truth and nothing but the truth. All knowledge is "perspectival" (Merleau-Ponty). There is always something of the perceiving and imagining subject in the description of the object known, no matter how scientific and objective that knowing pretends to be.

In the course of a lifetime, the human consciousness acquires a highly complex array of *images* and *perceptions* which act as patterns or programs central to this process of co-constituting reality.[3] These images and perceptions are a two-edged sword. Although they limit our grasp of what is, they also allow us to face life, get on with the business of living—more or less—and not be overwhelmed by the sheer immensity and unknowableness of what is. They allow us the "vital lies" of believing we have really grasped the truth. Life would be intolerable without such "lies"—that is why they are "vital."[4]

The danger is that we mistake these images and perceptions for what is, or at least, for what should be. Instead of being open to what is, constantly searching and submitting our images and perceptions to the more than and the beyond, always acknowledging the relativity of what we have grasped to this point, we may close down these possibilities—possibilities which make us truly human—and live with our programs and patterns as if we had already arrived where life is supposed to take us. Our images and perceptions of reality are "sacraments" of the Real. They ought to be constantly relinquished in favour of new and more helpful perceptions and images.

Clearly, not all images and perceptions act with the same power in our lives. Several factors can be noted which increase the significance of images and peceptions for individuals. At least one factor lending power to particular images and perceptions will be the *association*. Strong positive or negative or ambivalent associations can increase the influence significantly. The *context* within which the associations were made will also have some bearing (for example in family setting, in hospital, at school, etc.). More particuarly, the *function* these images and perceptions served will affect their influence. Finally, the *age* at which the image or perception gained its particular significance for the individual will be relevant.

IMAGES, FEELINGS, THOUGHTS, BEHAVIOR AND FREEDOM

Implicit in the foregoing is a certain chain of events: The kinds of images and perceptions that move in our consciousness will tend to affect—at times even determine—how we *feel*, what we *think* and how we *behave*. In other words, images and perceptions have a lot to do with our *freedom*.

Any of the authors referred to above could assist us in exploring this link. We will look at two authors not yet mentioned—A. Lazarus and R. Assagioli.[5] Lazarus writes:

> Words, ideas, values, attitudes, and beliefs are all replete with imagery. Find the images and you will understand the behavior. Furthermore, find the images and, if you so desire, you will probably be able to change the feelings and the behavior.[6]

Lazarus here not only highlights the significance of images but points to the possibility of change *of* and *through* them. In other words, we are not stuck with our images or the unfree behavior that results from them. Lazarus—and Ellis also—draws on the first century philosopher Epictetus who maintained:

> What disturbs men's minds is not events but their judgements on events . . . and so when we are hindered, or disturbed, or distressed, let us never lay the blame on others, but on ourselves, that is, on our own judgements.[7]

Assagioli suggests four "Laws" relating to the process:

> (Law I) . . . images or mental pictures and ideas tend to produce the physical conditions and the external acts that correspond to them.[8]
> (Law II) . . . attitudes, movements and actions tend to evoke corresponding images and ideas.[9]
> (Law III) . . . ideas and images tend to awaken emotions and feelings that correspond to them.[10]
> (Law IV) . . . emotions and impressions tend to awaken and intensify ideas and images that correspond to or are associated with them.[11]

UNDERSTANDING OUR IMAGES OF GOD

Applying the above to our issue of the images and perceptions we have of God, we could say, in general that:

- no one knows God as God is;
- everyone knows God by way of images and perceptions;
- these images and perceptions may assist or hinder our encounter with God as God is;
- when I reject or accept God it is reasonable to question whether I am rejecting or accepting God or a particular image or perception of God;
- these images and perceptions may be conscious or unconscious;
- our feeling and thinking about God and our behavior in view of

God will be significantly influenced by the images or perceptions we have of God;

- we can alter our feelings and thoughts about God and behavior in view of God by working to alter our images or perceptions of God.

It may be helpful to think in terms of *secondary* and *primary* images and perceptions. Perhaps we have multiple *secondary* images and perceptions of God but one *primary* image and perception. If that is the case, it would make sense to expect that *primary* one to be the key to the others, the one to be alert for if we wish to develop or change our images and perceptions of God. Furthermore, that *primary* image or perception may not be easily found. Using a personal journal, in conjunction with Eugene Gendlin's focusing techniques, perhaps conversations with a wise friend, disciplined study of sound teaching, and the normal practice of meditation and contemplation can assist the work of grace to take us beyond deformative and deforming images and perceptions and open up more creative possibilities.[12]

Where are some of the most basic images and perceptions of God, both formative and deformative, likely to come from? One of the more obvious sources is our *religious tradition*. For example, we may have been exposed to a rich experience of worship and liturgy, or we may have been subjected to very little that awakened the transcendent urgings in us; in our particular family the reality of God might have been quite strong, or it might have been more or less insignificant; our parents might have been more or less religious, irreligious or areligious; the preaching and teaching which we heard might have brought wholesome qualities—both human and divine—into focus, or it might have done the very opposite.

Another major source is the *cultural context* in which we find ourselves. For example, Australia has a largely irreligious history. Initially a convict settlement, more interested in sheer survival than values such as political and religious freedom, Australian society is now significantly dominated by functionalism, pragmatism and rationalism like the rest of the Western world. One wonders what influences other factors might have in any culture—factors like the weather, geography, isolation, abundance/lack of natural resources, language, consumerism, subsistence living, humanism, widespread availability or lack of availability of education, democratic/autocratic system of government, capitalist/socialist economics, association with other cultures (for example, indigenous populations), war, nuclear threat, affluence/poverty, and so on.

The *family environment* is clearly significant in the development of images and perceptions of God. For example, the presence or lack of religiosity, relationship with the institutional Church, the number of children, the physical and emotional health of family members, the relationship of parents with each other, our particular place in the family, the numbers of males/females and their respective roles, social status, expression of emotions, tensions, anxieties, values, place of residence, mobility, amount of money, closeness to extended family and so on.

Schooling may be more or less influential in facilitating the development of certain images and perceptions of God. For example, teachers, other students, size of school, place of school, punishments and rewards, atmosphere in the school, social consciousness, boarding or day, co-education or single sex, experience of religion classes and teachers, ability to cope with certain teaching and learning styles and so on.

Temperament might play a role in the images and perceptions of God that impress themselves upon us. For example, we may be artistic, emotionally sensitive, emotionally resilient, intelligent, extroverted, introverted, thoughtful, witty, logical, gregarious, and so on.

Personal events can have a lasting impression. For example, illness, happy marriage, broken marriage, car accident, near-death experience, culture shock, mystical experience, entering new phase of marital relationship, mid-life crisis, study, travel etc.

Significant people can bolster and change images and perceptions of God. For example, a mother or father, Mother Teresa, Jean Vanier, a dying child, a deeply holy person, a derelict, an arrogant "Christian," a person humbled by their own brokenness, a missionary working in a foreign land, and so on.

It could be objected that every forming influence is implicitly, at least, present in the foregoing. Biblical revelation reminds us that God is in our lives, the whole of our lives. The journey towards knowledge of self is also the journey towards knowledge of God, and vice versa. Our perceptions and images of God will be inextricably bound up with the general formation of our lives. In other words, God is in our religious tradition, in our cultural context, in our family upbringing, in our schooling, and so on. De facto, our images and perceptions of God will be implicitly or explicitly shaped by every experience of life. And, what is perhaps more important, if we have the consciousness that is permeated by faith, any experience—past, present or to come—can be creative in shaping images and perceptions of God that are freeing rather than binding.[13]

THE "APOPHATIC WAY" AND THE "KATAPHATIC WAY"

In the Jewish tradition there is a very deep respect for the ultimate unknowability of God. The very Name is kept secret to remind the community of the utter ineffability of God. Abraham Heschel writes well of "the ineffable name":

> The true name of God is a mystery. It is stated in the Talmud, "*And God said unto Moses . . . This is My name for ever* (Exodus 3:15). The Hebrew word 'for ever' (*leolam*) is written here in a way that it may be read *lealem* which means 'to conceal.' The name of God is to be concealed."
>
> Throughout the ages the Jews shrank from uttering, and, to some degree, even from writing out in full the four-lettered Holy Name of God (the Tetragrammaton). Except in the Bible, the name is usually not written out in full. Even when the portion of the Pentateuch is read during the service, the Name is never pronounced as it is written. The true name is the *Ineffable Name*. It is rendered by the Jews as *Adonai* (literally, "My Lord"), by the Samaritans as *Hashem*, and by the translators of the Bible into Greek by the word "Lord" (*kyrios*). According to Abba Saul, he who pronounces the Ineffable Name is among those who have no share in the life to come. "No one may utter the mystery of Thy name."
>
> Only once a year, on the Day of Atonement, was the Ineffable Name uttered by the High Priest at the Temple in Jerusalem. And when the name came out of his mouth, "in holiness and purity," "those who stood near him prostrated themselves, and those who stood afar said, 'Blessed be the name . . . for ever and ever.'" The name was pronounced ten times during the worship, and yet even before the people had left the Temple, all of them would forget the pronunciation. According to a medieval source, the name escaped even the High Priest himself as soon as he left the Temple.
>
> To this day the priests close their eyes when pronouncing the blessing, because when the Temple was in existence, they would utter the Ineffable Name . . . and the *Shechinah* would rest on their eyes. In remembrance thereof they close their eyes.

The Decalogue does not contain any commandment to worship God. It tells us "honor thy father and thy mother," it does not tell us, "honor thy God, worship Him, offer sacrifice to Him." The only reference to worship is indirect and negative: *"Thou shalt not take my name in vain."*[14]

In the Christian tradition two interrelated paths of knowing God have been explored by the great guides: the *via negativa* or the *apophatic way* and the *via positiva* or the *kataphatic way*. The former emphasizes God as essentially *unknowable*, and uses negations and silence to drive the point home. The latter emphasizes God as *knowable*, and uses affirmations and descriptive words and images to drive that point home. Both must be kept in creative tension in a healthy and lifegiving spirituality. Paradoxically each fosters the other—the more we know the more we know we don't know. Being human, earthy beings who create symbols, we must endeavour to create symbols that speak of the one from whom all life springs.

Dionysius the Areopagite (about the end of the fifth century) is the great Father of the apophatic way. And, in the final analysis, all attempts to know God must sooner or later come to that point of *not knowing*, the point of contemplation, silent wonder and mystical experience. Yet, in that very experience of *not knowing* we *know.*[15]

Our images and perceptions of God can bring us to this point of *not knowing* but no further. For God is *no-thing.* Language and experience point and we ponder. That language about God will always be "likey," "notty" and "morey." Whenever we affirm anything of God, we must do so with the understanding that what we are really saying is that God is *like* this, but God is *not* this, God is *more* than this. If we say "God is love," we are saying: "Consider love—not hate; look towards the horizon to which the concept of love orients your mind; God is that way; God is so much more than we can contemplate or imagine our puny expression 'love' to imply." Or again, if we say "God exists," we are saying: "Consider being, as distinct from non-being; look in that direction, ponder that; God cannot be contained in the tiny human concept of 'existence' though; God does not 'exist'; God breaks the boundaries of existence."

Thus, the great guides of the Christian tradition (for example, John of the Cross and Meister Eckhart) emphasize annihilation, renunciation, letting go, detachment and poverty. The way to know is the way to live: self-transcendence. The primary focus of knowing and living is beyond ourselves where our true center lies. The ego with all its images and perceptions is, as it were, a necessary illusion. Its whole purpose is to allow us to embark on the journey beyond it.

PRACTICAL SUGGESTIONS

1. Word association
   (a) Take a pen and paper to a quiet place.
   (b) Sit for a moment or two and be still.
   (c) Think of the word God and let associations emerge—images, events, symbols, people, words etc.
   (d) Write down what comes, free associating, following the connections, simply expressing and recording what is emerging—no matter how "irrelevant," "crazy," "disconnected" or "disconcerting" it may be. Pay particular attention to the feelings that come up.
   (e) When the flow of connections stops, sit and be still for a moment or two. Stay with the resulting "felt sense." Focus on that if you wish.
   (f) Reflect on what has emerged. Allow it to speak to you. What does it teach you? (Note: Do not try to "do" anything with it. Just take it in a matter of fact, non-judgmental way. Be with it and listen. Trust your spirit and the Holy Spirit to make something of it.)

2. Follow up
   (a) Some time after completing the word association exercise above, give some thought to the following kinds of questions:
   Does this shed any light on me and my thoughts, feelings and behavior?
   Are there any deformative images and perceptions operating here?
   Is there any lack of freedom here?
   Is there any one dominating influence here—perhaps an event, a person, a period of my life?
   Focus on what emerges, let it reveal what message it has.
   (b) Pray the simple prayer: "Into your hands I commend my spirit, Lord." Quietly state your situation and hand yourself over to the Lord just as you are.
   (c) Conclude by quietly praying one of your favorite Psalms or sit in silence.

3. Meditate on one of the following texts:
(a) Job 38–42;
(b) Psalm 8: "Yahweh our Lord, how majestic is your name throughout the world!" (NJB);
(c) Psalm 19: "The heavens declare the glory of God . . ." (NJB);
(d) Psalm 139: "Yahweh, you examine me and know me . . ." (NJB);
(e) 1Cor. 1:17–2:16: "What no eye has seen and no ear has heard . . ." (NJB).

Notes

1 Alice Walker, *The Color Purple*, Washington Square Press, 1982, pp.176–8.
2 "The Biblical man never asks: Is there a God?" (Abraham Heschel 1978, p.98.)
3 This is not to underestimate the power of the affective dimension in influencing the process of co-constituting reality. Affect and image/perception are inseparable and interdependent. See discussion below.
4 Cf. P. Berger and T. Luckmann 1966; G. Kelly 1955; A. Ellis and R. Harper 1975.
5 Cf. A. Lazarus 1977; Assagioli 1976 and 1977.
6 Op. cit., 35f.
7 Ibid.
8 Cf. Assagioli 1976, p.51.
9 Op. cit., p.52.
10 Op. cit., p.53.
11 Op. cit., p.54.
12 We should not underestimate both the urgency and the difficulty of working through the *emotional* experiences associated with deformative and deformed images and perceptions of God. They will almost certainly be intimately associated with similar images we have of ourselves. Their roots can be deep and complex. Working with them can be extremely painful. It is important to keep the focus clearly on the *experience*, listening attentively to that, and resisting the temptation to avoid that experience—probably because it is too threatening for one reason or another—and flee into judgment of "the other" (for example, "God," "father/mother," "Church," etc.).
13 For some further reading see: P. Solignac 1982; J. A. T. Robinson 1963; J. A. T. Robinson and D. L. Edwards 1963; H. Smith 1982; G. Hughes 1985; J. B. Phillips 1952, 1971. Is it possible that our images and perceptions of God have a mutuality with all our other images and perceptions: of ourselves, Church, other people, work, leisure, authority, family, etc.? Each in some way reflects the others? That we will in fact tend to feel, think and behave with respect to God as we feel, think and behave generally towards people, events and things and vice versa?
14 Abraham Heschel 1955/1978, pp.64f. See also Heschel 1951, pp.8f. This same theme is poignantly reflected in the words of Job: "Before I knew you only by hearsay but now having seen you with my own eyes, I retract what I have said, and repent in dust and ashes." (42:5f.—NJB)
15 Cf. St Gregory of Nyssa, "The Life of Moses"; Dionysius the Areopagite, *The Divine Names and the Mystical Theology*; H. A. Reinhold (ed.) 1973, 44-53; *The Cloud of Unknowing*; A. Greeley 1974, and E. Underhill 1915.

IMAGES OF GOD—THE MYSTERY BEYOND THE MYSTERY

'Come no nearer' he said. 'Take off your shoes for the place on which you stand is holy ground'. (Ex. 3:5–JB)

For God so loved the world that he gave his only Son, that whoever believes in him should not perish but have eternal life. (Jn. 3:16)

God raised him high and gave him the name which is above all other names so that all beings in the heavens, on earth and in the underworld should bend the knee at the name of Jesus and that every tongue should acclaim Jesus Christ as Lord, to the glory of God the Father. (Phil. 2:9–11–JB)

FACE TO FACE WITH THIS TERRIBLE REALITY

The images and perceptions we fabricate for God may or may not be helpful to us. At their best they point us in the right direction. They offer us a lookout from which we attend to a far horizon. At their worst they actually replace that for which they stand. Instead of serving a sacramental function in pointing beyond themselves they point to themselves. Instead of being transparent they become more or less opaque. And the images and perceptions are not to blame. We all have an immense capability for self-deception, for building walls between ourselves and the truth. Our perceptions and images can be just as easily ways of escape from reality as contact points with reality. And we are very good at rationalizing it when we are caught out.

For most of us, truth—especially ultimate truth—does not even begin to come into view with any power until we have been brought low. There is nothing like an experience of ego desperation to make us look with seriousness for that which is real. The Spanish philosopher Ortega describes this well:

All the matters about which science speaks, whatever the science be, are abstract, and abstract things are always clear. So that the clarity of science is not so much in the heads of scientists as in the matters of which they speak. What is really confused, intricate, is the concrete vital reality, always a unique thing. The man who is capable of steering a clear course through it, who can perceive under the chaos presented by every vital situation the hidden anatomy of the movement, the man, in a word, who does not lose himself in life, that is the man with the really clear head. Take stock of those around you and you will see them wandering about lost through life, like sleep-walkers in the midst of their good or evil fortune, without the slightest suspicion of what is happening to them. You will hear them talk in precise terms about themselves and their surroundings, which would seem to point to them having ideas on the matter. But start to analyze those ideas and you will find that they hardly reflect in any way the reality to which they appear to refer, and if you go deeper you will discover that there is not even an attempt to adjust the ideas to this reality. Quite the contrary: through these notions the individual is trying to cut off any personal vision of reality, of his own very life. For life is at the start a chaos in which one is lost. The individual suspects this, but he is frightened at finding himself face to face with this terrible reality, and tries to cover it over with a curtain of fantasy, where everything is clear. It does not worry him that his "ideas" are not true, he uses them as trenches for the defence of his existence, as scarecrows to frighten away reality. The man with the clear head is the man who frees himself from those fantastic "ideas" and looks life in the face, realizes that everything in it is problematic and feels himself lost. As this is the simple truth—that to live is to feel oneself lost—he who accepts it has already begun to find himself, to be on firm ground. Instinctively, as do the shipwrecked, he will look round for something to which to cling, and that tragic, ruthless glance, absolutely sincere, because it is a question of his salvation, will cause him to bring order into the chaos of his life. These are the only genuine ideas; the ideas of the shipwrecked. All the rest is rhetoric, posturing, farce. He who does not really feel himself lost is lost without remission; that is to say, he never finds himself, never comes up against his own reality.[1]

Genuine artists typically bear the burden of being aware of "this terrible reality." Often enough their lives bear the marks of "the shipwrecked" too. They are, as it were, blessed with the curse of seeing reality a good deal more clearly than the rest of us. Graham Greene was such a person. Nowhere is this more evident than his classic novel, *The Power and the Glory*. When the lieutenant has finally captured the whisky priest, he endeavors to understand the priest and his belief, even as he professes contempt for those beliefs. In one of their exchanges the whisky priest offers a startling insight into God that is all the more compelling because it is spoken by a truly "shipwrecked" man:

> They lay quiet for a while in the hut. The priest thought the lieutenant was asleep until he spoke again. "You never talk straight. You say one thing to me—but to another man, or a woman, you say, 'God is love.' But you think that stuff won't go down with me, so you say different things. Things you'll know I'll agree with."
> "Oh," the priest said, "that's another thing altogether—God *is* love. I don't say the heart doesn't feel a taste of it, but what taste. The smallest glass of love mixed with a pint pot of ditch water. We wouldn't recognize *that* love. It might even look like hate. It would be enough to scare us—God's love. It set fire to a bush in the desert, didn't it, and smashed open graves and set the dead to walking in the dark. Oh, a man like me would run a mile to get away if he felt that love around."[2]

THE REVELATION OF GOD IN TRADITION

It is possible for us who adhere to the Judeo-Christian tradition to miss something of the richness of our own tradition because we are ignorant of other traditions. Furthermore, belief in the truth of the specifically Christian revelation does not necessarily mean that we deny that God is also truly revealed in the other great religious traditions.[3]

There are certain common elements that keep recurring in the attempts of the human family to address the ultimate desires of the heart, to seek the meaning and purpose of human existence, to understand the one, the true, the good and the beautiful, to respond quite naturally to the sheer awesomeness of creation in its manifold forms.[4]

Aelred Squire sets the context for understanding both what the Christian tradition reveals about God and what we ourselves might discover of God by encountering that tradition through its texts—especially the Bible:

> We too often fail to realize that one of the primary purposes of holy Scripture, considered as a vital whole, is to show man to himself, as he was made and as he has become, as he acts and reacts in relation to his maker, with *nothing* left out. Hence the violence and crudity and sensuality that God there pushes in front of our noses, even if we would, to our very great danger, prefer to turn away. The God of the

Bible does not whittle down the truth, and we must not try to do so either. Then, beside these mirrors, universal in their validity, there are others for our more particular information, held up to us by those in the past or the present whose development we are personally best prepared to understand and, surer still, those additional portraits of ourselves we are daily making in the actions and thoughts which mirror what we individually are. Even those who imagine they know themselves will often be surprised at what they see, if they have the courage to look honestly into *those* mirrors. From those, particularly, we shall often prefer to look away. But from time to time, in a moment of grace, which we can either accept or refuse, we shall be forced to look, and then we shall either be humbled and led back to the God of inexorable truth, or turn angrily away and lose ourselves in lies.

Yet the living Truth, the great breaker of idols and destroyer of false Gods, is ultimately easier to live with than the most comforting of lies. It is better to lose the God we found it easy to envisage, and the faith that was only a protection from our fears, and stand naked and unknowing in the presence of the One who can only really be known when he is lived with. At least with that God we can and, indeed, must begin from where we are. There can be no becoming which does not start from something that really is.[5]

Gregory of Nyssa (c.335–c.395) is a good representative of the Christian tradition. Gregory, particularly in his *Life of Moses*, presents a clearly articulated description of how the Christian develops in knowledge of God. He suggests a threefold movement through experiences of "light" (when we first begin to take the call of the Gospel seriously), "cloud" (when we have undergone a good deal of purification and begun to enter the realm of mysticism; Gregory speaks here of "the feelings of presence") and "darkness" (when we enter into a deeper knowledge of the transcendence and incomprehensibility of God).[6]

For Gregory there is no opposition between "nature" and "supernature."[7] The whole purpose of human existence may be seen in terms of "the restoration of the image of God in man."[8] We become what the story of Adam and Eve reveals that we are made to be: companions of God. Following Origen—and later reflected repeatedly in the tradition, especially Bernard of Clairvaux—Gregory stresses freedom, more than intelligence, as the central mark of "the image and likeness."[9] To choose to submit to grace so that the image of God might be restored is the most complete expression of each person's vocation. Gregory writes: "The true satisfaction of (the soul's) desire consists in constantly going on with her quest and never ceasing in her quest."[10]

In Gregory we have an image and perception of God that is *full of energy*. Gregory has taken seriously and with absolute faith the revelation of Scripture: We are made in the image and likeness of Life itself, our whole being cries out for the full restoration of that reality, God has heard that cry for freedom and meets it with the utmost prodigality. God is the eternal and personal Mystery in whom we find the Energies of existence and the more we become caught up in those Energies, the more we become "inebriated" with Life.[11]

REVELATION OF GOD IN THE COVENANTS

We have already noted the centrality of the Exodus event and Covenant in the OT and the Passover event and Covenant—"New Exodus" and "New Covenant"—of the NT.[12] All that is revealed in the OT and NT finds its meaning and purpose, directly or indirectly, by reference to these two pivotal events.

In the OT a central text giving us access to the revelation of God in the Covenant is Exodus 3:1–15—the revelation of God to Moses on Horeb. Whatever else we say about this revelation, it is not a clearcut definition or even description of God. It is rather a pointer. John Courtney Murray writes:

> In the enigmatic play on words and in the Name Yahweh that embodies its sense, Moses and his people heard not the affirmation that God is or that he is Creator but the promise that he would be present with his people. God's utterance of his Name is to be understood in the light of the promise to Moses that precedes it ("I will be with you") and which in another form follows it: "I will help you to speak, and I will tell you what you have to say" (Ex. 4:12). The sense of the verb "to be" is relational, or intersubjective. For the ancient Israelites, as for all primitive peoples, existence was an affair of community; to be was to be-with-the-others. Existence was also an effective affair; to be was to be-in-action. Finally, existence was of the phenomenal, not the essential, order; to be was to be-there, concretely and in evidence.
> One might translate: "I shall be there as who I am shall I be there." The text, thus understood, contains a threefold revelation—of God's immanence in history, of his transcendence to history, and of his transparency through history. God first asserts the fact of his presence

LIVING STRINGS

in the history of his people: "I shall be there." Second, he asserts the mystery of his own being: "I shall be there as who I am." His mystery is a mode of absence. Third, he asserts that, despite his absence in mystery, he will make himself known to his people: "As who I am shall I be there." The mode of his transparency is through his action, through the saving events of the sacred history of Israel.[13]

In the actual description of the Covenant of Sinai[14] the revelation of that "mystery presence" is further elaborated. Three key words are used: *rahamim, hesed* and *emet*. The first two words emphasize the "presence" as full of compassion, tender loving kindness, mercy, pity, freely chosen by God. The last word emphasizes the faithfulness of that "presence."[15]

The overwhelming sense is of a profoundly personal, life-giving, loving and liberating "mystery presence" who will never forsake this people chosen in pure graciousness. Both the absolute transcendence and the radical immanence are maintained in tension. There is nothing simply remote or capricious about this "mystery presence." The revelation says very clearly: "I am freedom and love, I am on your side, I shall always be with you to share my freedom and love."

This is a personal and relational God, one whose identity for us is, as it were, incomplete unless we choose to respond and enter the relationship in the same spirit in which it was graciously initiated: in freedom and love. In loving we know. This revelation does not give us a definition so much as an invitation: enter the loving conversation, let your heart be touched, and you will know richly the unknowable, understand clearly the incomprehensible.[16]

In the NT Jesus is revealed as the incarnation of the Covenant. His name is "God with us" ("Emmanuel") and his name *is* his being and his doing. The revelation of God in the first Covenant is confirmed and further extended in the New Covenant. The absolute transcendence is confirmed and further revealed in Jesus' power over the forces of darkness, most particularly manifested in his conquest of death. The radical immanence is revealed and further revealed in Jesus' humanity, most particularly manifested in his *kenosis*—his following the human journey to its darkest limits through Gethsemane and Calvary.[17]

Throughout the OT and NT there are numerous revelations of God through stories, historical events, people and prayerful outpourings. Any or all of those further revelations can only be understood as *subsequent* and *subsidiary* to the primary revelation in the Covenants. Thus, God is

"Creator";[18] "Law maker";[19] "Adversary";[20] "Comforting Mother";[21]; "Lover";[22] "Jilted Husband";[23] "Powerful Warrior";[24] "Punisher";[25] "Rewarder";[26] "Healer";[27] "Glorious One";[28] "Suffering Servant";[29] "Eternal Word";[30] "Reconciler";[31] And so on.

PRACTICAL SUGGESTIONS

Spend some time meditating on any one or all of the following texts:

"I do not think one can ever conceive a loving God as a God of final reprobation, in the sense that a man (or an angel) is shut out from him for ever. What can be thought is a loving God whose love is absolutely terrifying in its relentless pressure." (N. D. O'Donoghue 1979, p.141, from the essay "The Faces of God")

"We shall be in a position to hear the voice of the Good Shepherd only when we have stopped using the Christian religion to shield us from the realities of our lostness and our night." (D. J. Hall 1979, pp.254–67)

"Notice that in the Gospels there is never, unless I am mistaken, question of a search for God by man. In all the parables it is the Christ who seeks men, or else the Father has them fetched by His messengers. Or again, a man finds the Kingdom of God as if by chance, and then, but then only, he sells all." (S. Weil (1952) 1987, p.1)

"I take this opportunity of acquainting you with the opinions of one of our friars upon the consequences and helps that have resulted from his practice of the presence of God. Let us both profit by them. You know that his principal aim during more than forty years 'in religion' has been to be always with God and neither to do, say nor think anything which might displease Him: and this without any other object but love, the most meritorious of considerations. He has now made such a habit of this practice that he receives divine assistance at all times and places; and for about thirty years his soul has been excited by interior joys, so continuous and so overpowering that, to prevent them being manifest outwardly, he has had to take refuge in behaviour that savours more of silliness than of sanctity." (Brother Lawrence (1931) 1977, p.55)

Notes

1 José Ortega y Gasset (1932) 1960, pp.156f.
2 Graham Greene 1982, pp.199–200.
3 Cf. Vatican II "Declaration of the Relationship of the Church to Non-Christian Religions" and "Declaration on Religious Freedom."
4 Cf. for example Rudolph Otto 1958; Huston Smith 1965; Ninian Smart 1964.
5 A. Squire 1973, 10f.

6   Cf. Gregory of Nyssa 1978, pp.94–6. See also Jean Danielou 1961, pp.23-33. In developing his description in this threefold way, Gregory draws on the experience of Moses: "Moses' vision of God began with light; afterwards God spoke to him in a cloud. But when Moses rose higher and became more perfect, he saw God in the darkness." (J. Danielou, op. cit., p.23)

7   Cf. op. cit., 11.

8   Op. cit., p.10.

9   Op. cit., p.12.

10 Cited by Danielou, op. cit., p.26.

11 Cf. op. cit., pp.33–46. It would be an interesting personal exercise to search the spiritual classics for images and perceptions of God. In different ways, the thought of Gregory—"the father of Christian mysticism"—recurs again and again. The English writers have a gentleness about their perception (cf. E. Colledge, *Medieval Mystics of England*). Bernard of Clairvaux has a certain passion, sometimes deeply affectionate, sometimes bordering on the harsh (cf. for example, Brian P. McGuire 1991, 17–42). Meister Eckhart is Zen-like (cf. for example, his *Sermons*). Teresa of Avila is a powerful mixture of passion and hard-headed realism (cf. for example, her *Autobiography* or *The Interior Castle*). Similarly Teresa's close friend, John of the Cross (cf. for example, *The Ascent of Mount Carmel* or *The Living Flame of Love*). And so on.

12 Cf. Chapter 2.

13 J. C. Murray 1964, 9f.

14 Cf. Ex. 19–34.

15 Cf. for example, Ex. 33:18–34:9.

16 For a good discussion of the God of Biblical revelation as distinct from the God of the Greek philosophical tradition, see A. Heschel 1975, pp.1–47; William Barret (1958) 1962, pp.69–91. Gregory of Nyssa says: "This is the true knowledge of what is sought; this is seeing that consists in not seeing, because that which is sought transcends all knowledge, being separated on all sides by incomprehensibility as by a kind of darkness. Wherefore John the sublime, who penetrated into the luminous darkness, says, *No one has ever seen God* (Jn. 1:18), thus asserting that knowledge of the divine essence is unattainable not only by men but also by every intelligent creature." (Gregory of Nyssa, op. cit., p.95)

17 St. Paul highlights both the transcendence and immanence of God as revealed in Jesus Christ in Phil. 2:6ff.

18 For example, Gen. 1:1–31.

19 For example, Ex. 20:1–21 & Mt. 5:20–48.

20 For example, Gen. 32:23–32.

21 For example, Is. 66:12–13.

22 For example, Song of Songs.

23 For example, Hos. 2:1–24.

24 For example, Ps. 144.

25 For example, Gen. 6:4–12 & Mt. 23:13–36.

26 For example, Mt. 6:5–6.

27 For example, Mt. 9:1–8.

28 For example, Dan. 7:9–14 & Mk. 9:2–8.

29 For example, Is. 42:1ff. etc. & Mt. 12:18–21.

30 For example, Jn. 1:1f.

31 For example, Lk. 15:11–32. There is no single image or perception of God in the Bible that covers all the possibilities. There are literally dozens of images and perceptions. It may be a useful exercise to reflect on some of those not already mentioned above and let them affect you. Reflect on your spontaneous reactions. And do not forget the seminal revelation of the Covenants.

8

THE BIBLE AS TRAGEDY

The years of our life are threescore and ten, or even by reason of strength fourscore; yet their span is but toil and trouble; they are soon gone, and we fly away. Who considers the power of thy anger, and thy wrath according to the fear of thee? So teach us to number our days that we may get a heart of wisdom. (Ps. 90:10–12)

And he said to all, 'If any man would come after me, let him deny himself and take up his cross daily and follow me. For whoever would save his life will lose it; and whoever loses his life for my sake, he will save it. For what does it profit a man if he gains the whole world and loses or forfeits himself?' (Lk. 9:23–5)

For since, in the wisdom of God, the world did not know God through wisdom, it pleased God through the folly of what we preach to save those who believe. For Jews demand signs and Greeks seek wisdom, but we preach Christ crucified, a stumbling block to Jews and folly to Gentiles, but to those who are called, both Jews and Greeks, Christ the power of God and the wisdom of God. (1Cor. 1:21–4)

A DOMESTIC SITUATION

Good literature always has at least a touch of tragedy to it. It is not always the focus, nor is it always explicit. But it is always there, at least implicitly. Fairytales are riddled with tragedy. Shakespeare's King Lear is both one of the finest plays ever written and one of the great tragedies.[1] Contemporary novels and plays are frequently heavily laden with tragedy.[2]

Contemporary American novelist John Gardner provides us with a good example. He describes a quarrel between a husband and wife that intimates the tragic dimension of life in its most mundane, domestic form.[3] She has just been to the doctor who has told her that, should she have children, they would almost certainly be blind. She rages at her husband. He accepts it gently and mildly, which makes her even more angry. She even thought of killing herself, as a way of getting even with him. Later that night the horrible truth of it all dawns on her—it is not her husband she hates, it is life. Life, the concrete form of condemning her to be either childless or to have children who are disabled. The non-negotiable harshness of life has left her feeling awfully impotent.

Good literature always has the tragic domain either just off stage or right on stage because that is the way human existence is. The particularities of Fred and Esther's life might be different from yours and mine. But the bottom line is not far removed from our experience.[4] Esther's quarrel is not ultimately with Fred. No quarrel is ever ultimately what it seems on the surface, never with this or that person in the end. Every quarrel is ultimately a quarrel with life. "Life should not be like this!" "This should not have happened to me!" Perhaps our quarrel is not even with life but with God.[5]

Thus, in literature as in life, love can give birth to resentment, the longing for life throws us up against death, laughter mingles with tears, triumph and failure are two sides of the one coin. Every blessing is a curse, every curse a blessing. Life does not give us what we want so we turn on ourselves and those around us, employing our best energies and talents to strike back, or "play games," or withdraw. We blame and curse, we feel disappointed and despondent, we hide in cynicism and indifference, we sigh and weep, and, if we are blessed, seek forgiveness and healing. Then we go on with the journey, better prepared—perhaps—for the next time we meet life in this guise.

WHAT IS TRAGEDY?

With what kinds of human experiences do we associate the word "tragedy"?[6] Mostly it is death—literal or metaphorical. It is tragic, for example, when a young mother is killed in a car accident, when a talented and otherwise healthy young man contracts AIDS, when intelligent adults employ their abilities to deceive and hurt people, when young men and women fritter away their lives in fear of commitment.

Our response may run the gamut of emotions, from profound sadness and grief, through disappointment and disbelief, to fear and anger. Underlying them all is an existential anxiety. Existence and non-existence are the issues here. As one of the well known tragic figures of literature put it: "To be or not to be." Unless we are particularly deadened, the experience of tragedy will not leave us unmoved.[7]

Tragedy is that moment when life and death seem to become one. The boundaries between them disappear or simply become confused and death, or the echoes of death, invades life with an ease that terrifies us. The invasion reminds us that death can and might do that at any time.

The ancients were aware of this. In their mythologies *Thanatos* always shadowed *Eros*. They knew that life and death are organically linked.

Rollo May suggests that we have forgotten this truth and our forget-fulness becomes especially evident in our obsession with romantic love. Thus, the otherwise healthy and lifegiving experience of "falling in love" may become a primary means of avoiding both the healthy and the lifegiving:

> When we *fall* in love, as the expressive verb puts it, the world shakes and changes around us . . . The shaking generally is felt consciously in its positive aspects—as a wonderful new universe which love, with its miracle, suddenly has produced. Love is the answer, we sing. But our Western culture seems to be engaged in a desperate—albeit romantic—conspiracy to enforce the illusion that this is *all* there is to eros. The very strength of the effort to support the illusion betrays the strong presence of the repressed, opposing pole.
>
> This element we deny is the consciousness of death. For death is always in the shadow of the light of love. In the shadows, too, is the dread, haunting question: will this new relationship destroy us? When we love, we give up the centre of ourselves. We are thrown from our previous state of existence into a void, and though we hope for a new world, and for a new existence, we can never be sure. Nothing looks the same and may never look the same again. Our world is annihilated. How can we know whether it will ever be built up again? We give, and we give up, our own centre. How shall we know that we will get it back? We wake to find the whole world shaking. Where or when will it come to rest?
>
> The most excruciating joy is accompanied by the consciousness of the imminence of death—and with the same intensity. And it seems that one is not possible without the other.[8]

Another element of tragedy arises out of the part we play as free agents.[9] The ultimate tragedies are those *caused* by free choices. The tragic is part and parcel of life, whether we choose it, abet it, oppose it, humbly suffer it, or ignore it. But when we use our gifts of freedom and consciousness to thwart life's possibilities—and thus invite death in—we become the agents of tragedy in a special way.

Implicit in this collusion with the tragic is the subtle evil of goodness turned against itself. Evil has no power of its own—it needs goodness to do its work. The tragic dimension of life is at its most poignant when it arises from the best intentions and we employ our best energies, talents and possibilities as the instruments of our own demise. Far from breaking free of the clutches of death, life engages life in a battle unto death. The good becomes its own enemy, the possible gives birth to the impossible.[10]

This is the final irony of life perhaps. Tragedy, whether it comes upon us or we bring it upon ourselves, leaves us unfulfilled but yearning and longing more than ever for life—life which is tragic. That yearning and longing, however, may be subverted by overwhelming feelings of sadness, depression, nothingness, emptiness, despair and despondency. Tragedy gouges the human spirit and that gouging can open us up to the greater potential implicit in the heart's longing or it can simply crush us. Whether it is life or death that fills the craters depends on the choices we make.[11]

OUR RESPONSE TO TRAGEDY

On the face of it, the presence of the tragic dimension in life ought to lead us to despair. Maybe Sartre is right—life is absurd. We might be able to summon our strengths and survive a tragic event. Can we survive the knowledge that *life itself* is tragic? We can rightly object that life is not *only* tragic.[12] But if we deny that it is tragic we will find ourselves living a lie, spending much energy evading those voices that call us more deeply into the truth of who, what and why we are.[13]

One of the most bewildering and inspiring paradoxes of tragedy is that many people face it, live it, and become more deeply human through it. Show me a compassionate and merciful person and I will show you someone who knows tragedy firsthand.[14]

The very qualities that dispose us to tragedy—our spiritual nature and in particular our freedom and consciousness—are the same qualities that allow us to respond to tragedy creatively. Tragedy can be an opening to the Real in a way that no other human experience can be.[15]

Throughout the Bible tragedy comes and goes like the ubiquitous face of life that it is. The biblical authors do not tell tragic stories for effect. They tell tragic stories because they want to express what is and what happens in the human story. The Bible is a microcosm of the human story as such.[16]

The story of Adam and Eve is perhaps the most potent and insightful representation of the tragic dimension of human existence. Life and death intermingle, great promise becomes great threat, deep and wonderful yearning becomes the superficial and sad servant of pride, at-homeness with God, self and world is the seed bed of conflict and alienation, freedom is the source of bondage.

Cain kills Abel.[17] A pathetic story of domestic envy. The peoples of the earth build a tower, symbol of their talent and their arrogance, and end up babbling at each other.[18] The wonderful saga of Abraham evokes a deep sense of the tragic.[19] He and Sarah exhibit great faith and trust in the Lord as they tread their pilgrim path.

And so it goes. Person after person. Event after event. In every single book of the Old Testament tragedy makes an appearance in one form or another, until the great tragic figure of human history: Jesus of Nazareth. One contemporary author sums up the reality of Jesus and his message well when writes for preachers of the Word:

> The pressure on the preacher of course is to speak just the answer. The answer is what people have come to hear and what he has also come to hear, preaching always as much to himself as to anybody, to keep his spirits up. He has to give an answer because everybody else is giving answers. Transcendental meditation is an answer, and the Democratic party is an answer, or the Republican party, and acupuncture and acupressure are answers, and so are natural foods, yogurt, and brown rice. Yoga is an answer and transactional analysis and jogging. The pressure on the preacher is to promote the Gospel, to sell Christ as an answer that outshines all the other answers by talking up the shining side, by calling even the day of his death Good Friday when if it was good, it was good only after it was bad, the worst of all Fridays. The pressure is to be a public relations man, and why not, only not to the neglect of private relations, the relations especially of a man with God and with God less as a presence much of the time than as an absence, an empty place where grace and peace belong. The preacher has to be willing to speak as tragic a word as Jesus speaks, which is the word that even if all the problems that can be solved are solved—poverty, war, ignorance, injustice, disease—and even if all the answers the world can give are proved each in its own way workable, even so man labors and is heavy laden in his helplessness; poor naked wretch that bides the pelting of the storm that is no less pitiless for all the preaching of all the preachers.[20]

The greatest story ever told includes us as major players—"All of us who have been baptized into Christ Jesus were baptized into his death."[21] And the resounding message of it all is *faith, hope and love grounded in the True and the Real.*

The Bible does not invent tragedy, or tell of it because the authors have a morbid streak. The Bible tells of life! And the path to life—deep life—is tragic. "Blessed are those who mourn, for they shall be comforted."[22] We are able to live with life as tragic without becoming cynical or despairing because of Christ. Tragedy gives birth to life. Easter Day demanded Good Friday. No tragedy, no life—and that's the essence of the tragic. It should really be otherwise. But it is not.

> Truly, truly, I say to you, unless a grain of wheat falls into the earth and dies, it remains alone; but if it dies, it bears much fruit. He who loves his life loses it, and he who hates his life in this world will keep it for eternal life.[23]

PRACTICAL SUGGESTIONS

a) Consider your reaction to the discussion of the tragic above. Write down your thoughts and feelings in a non-judgmental and unedited way. What is happening?

b) Can you think of any great—or even notorious—person in history who has not, in some way, been associated with tragedy? Even the best of them come down to us as ambivalent characters, inextricably tied to the human family in its painful struggles to live in this "land of unlikeness" we call the human condition.

c) Part of feeling secure is a sense of meaning and purpose in life. Yet, part of being deeply mature is learning to live with the fact that we can never feel utterly secure here, never know with any certitude the meaning and purpose of life. Meditate on the following statements by two contemporary authors. Do they express anything of your own experience?

> My Lord God, I have no idea where I am going. I do not see the road ahead of me. I cannot know for certain where it will end. Nor do I really know myself, and the fact that I think I am following your will does not mean that I am actually doing so. But I believe that the desire to please you does in fact please you. And I hope that I do not do anything apart from that desire. And I know that if I do this you will lead me by the right road, though I may know nothing about it. Therefore I will trust you always though I may seem to be lost and in the shadow of death. I will not fear, for you are ever with me, and you will never leave me to face my perils alone.[24]
>
> My God I don't love you, and I don't even want to because I am bored with you. Perhaps I don't even believe in you. But look at me as you go by! Take shelter for a moment in my soul and set it in order with a breath, without seeming to, without saying anything to me. If you want

me to believe in you bring some faith. If you want me to love you bring me some love. As for me I haven't any and there is nothing I can do about it. I can only give you what I've got, my weakness and my grief. And this tenderness that torments me and that you can surely see . . . and this despair . . . this maddening shame. My pain, nothing but my pain! That's all. And my hope.[25]

Notes

1   For an excellent contemporary novel based on the themes of *King Lear*, see Jane Smiley, *A Thousand Acres*.

2   This would be particularly true of writers like Camus and Sartre. It is also true, to varying degrees, of Graham Greene, Shusaku Endo, Flannery O'Connor, Patrick White, Herman Melville, Henry James, Mary Gordon, Jane Smiley, Eudora Welty, Arthur Miller, Saul Bellow, Kurt Vonnegut and many others.

3   J. Gardner, *The Sunlight Dialogues*, pp.305–8.

4   Perhaps Freud himself was saying precisely this when he further developed his thought to include a death instinct in the light of the wholesale tragedy of World War I. Ernest Becker recalls: "Freud summed it up beautifully when he somewhere remarked that psychoanalysis cured the neurotic misery in order to introduce the patient to the common misery of life." (Becker 1973, p.57).

5   Note Simone Weil's observation: "Amid the multitude of those who seem to owe us something, God is our only real debtor. But our debt to him is greater. He will release us from it if we forgive him. Sin is an offence offered to God from resentment at the debts he owes and does not pay us. By forgiving God we cut the root of sin in ourselves. At the bottom of every sin there is anger against God. If we forgive God for his crime against us, which is to have made us finite creatures, he will forgive our crimes against him, which is that we are finite creatures." (Simone Weil in G. Panichas 1973, p.433).

6   This very question provides us with a good example of the confusion over language experienced in Western society. For example, if a sporting star is unable to play for the team in the final it is a "tragedy"! I suggest we try to retrieve the word from this kind of trivialization.

7   In wartime, for example, a soldier probably will not experience the tragedy of the violent death of another human being if that human being happens to be "the enemy." He or she has a vested interest, psychologically, in not experiencing that as tragedy. It would undermine their ability to go on fighting. Also, soldiers might not experience the tragedy of a fallen comrade in the heat of battle. Again psychological survival mechanisms will tend to protect them. Those who do not have such mechanisms of repression available to them will almost certainly disintegrate emotionally on the spot. Others may disintegrate later.

8   Rollo May 1968, p.19. May goes on to note: "The relationship between death and love certainly is clear in the sex act. Every kind of mythology relates the sex act itself to dying . . . What a different light this throws on the human problems in love than does all our glib talk about the art of loving, about love as the answer to all our needs, love as instant self-actualization, love as contentment, or love as a mailorder technique! No wonder we try to reduce eros to purely physiological sex or try to avoid the whole dilemma by playing it cool, by using sex to drug and vaccinate ourselves against the anxiety-creating effects of eros." (p.20). Contemporary author Annie Dillard approaches the same reality from another point of view: "I don't know what it is about fecundity that so appals. I suppose it is the teeming evidence that birth

and growth, which we value, are ubiquitous and blind, that life itself is so astonishingly cheap, that nature is as careless as it is bountiful, and that with extravagance goes a crushing waste that will one day include our own cheap lives ... Every glistening egg is a memento mori." (1974, p.160).

9   Only human beings experience tragedy. Pigs, for example, do not know tragedy. Without some intimations of the grand calling of the human being, we would not be able to know tragedy either.

10   Paul Tillich says "the law of tragedy turns the attempts to strengthen the good into a strengthening of evil." (1948, p.187).

11   In his Commentary on John's Gospel (40, 10), St Augustine says "it is yearning that makes the heart deep." St John of the Cross speaks of "the deep caverns" that are the soul's faculties and these "caverns" must be "emptied, purged, and cleansed of every affection for creature, (otherwise) they do not feel the vast emptiness of their deep capacity." ("The Living Flame of Love," 18, translation by Kieran Kavanagh and Otilio Rodriguez) Contemporary novelist Saul Bellow writes: "We are all drawn towards the same craters of the spirit—to know what we are and to know what we are for, to know our purpose, to seek grace. And, if the quest is the same, the differences in our personal histories, which hitherto meant so much to us, become of minor importance." (1944/1988, p.154).

12   Life can be described in many ways. For example, life is also comic. We will focus on that aspect in Chapter 9.

13   Ortega's comment is blunt and to the point: "Every destiny is dramatic, tragic in its deepest meaning." (1957, p.21). The tendency to deny the tragic side of human existence may be particularly prevalent in the Western world today. One author, reviewing Wendy Kaminer's book *I'm Dysfunctional, You're Dysfunctional: The Recovery Movement and Other Self-Help Fashions*, comments: "We don't put much stock in failure, limitation or uncertainty; these are just transient states or problems to be solved, shells, appearances. According to the recovery movement, evil, as Ms. Kaminer puts it, 'is merely a mask—a dysfunction.' If you build enough self-confidence and train hard, if you follow the right regimen, you can recapture your original glory. Such beliefs ... don't really tell one much about how to live with pain or loss or an uncertain future." (Miller 1992, p.44).

14   For example: "How wonderfully is man's love transformed by the interior experience of this nothingness and this nowhere. . . . He who patiently abides in this darkness will be comforted and feel again a confidence about his destiny, for gradually he will see his past sins healed by grace. The pain continues yet he knows it will end, for even now it grows less intense. Slowly he begins to realise that the suffering he endures is not hell at all but his purgatory." (Cloud of Unknowing, 1973, p.137.)

    "To see the infinite pity of this place./ The mangled limb, the devastated face,/ The innocent sufferers, smiling at the rod;/ A fool were tempted to deny his God;/ He sees, and shrinks, but if he look again,/ Lo, beauty springing from the breast of pain,/ He marks the sisters on the painful shores,/ And even a fool is silent and adores." (Robert Louis Stevenson, after a visit to the leper colony at Kalaupapa, Molokai, 1888. A framed copy of this poem is on the wall of the hospital at Kalaupapa.)

15   Maria Boulding's wonderful little book, *Gateway to Hope: An Exploration of Failure* (Fount Paperbacks, 1985), is well worth careful reading in this context.

16   Do you know any extended family that has not been touched in some way by the tragic dimension of life? Is it possible that some marriages fail because the people involved expect, perhaps implicitly, that their relationship will avoid the tragic dimension of life?

17   Gen. 4:1ff. "Now Adam knew Eve his wife, and she conceived and bore Cain, saying, "I have gotten a man with the help of the Lord. And again, she bore his brother Abel.

Now Abel was a keeper of sheep, and Cain a tiller of the ground. In the course of time Cain brought to the Lord an offering of the fruit of the ground, and Abel brought of the firstlings of his flock and of their fat portions. And the Lord had regard for Abel and his offering, but for Cain and his offering he had no regard. So Cain was very angry, and his countenance fell. . . ."

18   Gen. 11:1ff "Now the whole earth had one language and few words. And they said to one another, 'Come, let us make bricks, and burn them thoroughly.' And they had brick for stone, and bitumen for mortar. Then they said, 'Come, let us build ourselves a city, and a tower with its top in the heavens, and let us make a name for ourselves, lest we be scattered abroad upon the face of the whole earth.' And the Lord said, 'Behold, they are one people, and they have all one language; and this is only the beginning of what they will do; and nothing that they propose to do will now be impossible for them. Come, let us go down, and there confuse their language, that they may not understand one another's speech.' Therefore its name was called Ba'bel, because there the Lord confused the language of all the earth; and from there the Lord scattered them abroad over the face of all the earth."

19   Cf. Gen. 12:1ff.

20   Frederick Buechner 1977, p.35f. Miguel de Unamuno writes: "Jews and Greeks each arrived independently at the real discovery of death—a discovery which occasions, in peoples as in men, the entrance into spiritual puberty, the realization of the tragic sense of life, and it is then that the living God is begotten by humanity. The discovery of death is that which reveals God to us, and the death of the perfect man, Christ, was the supreme revelation of death, being the death of the man who ought not to have died yet did die." (1968, p.75).

21   Rom. 6:3. Note also Paul's words to the Corinthians: "For as often as you eat this bread and drink the cup, you proclaim the Lord's death until he comes." 1Cor. 11:26

22   Mt. 5:4.

23   Jn. 12:24f.

24   Thomas Merton 1958, p.83.

25   Marie Noel 1968, p.29.

9
THE BIBLE AS COMEDY

*God said, " . . . Sarah your wife shall bear you a son, and you shall call his name Isaac.
I will establish my covenant with him as an everlasting covenant for his descendants
after him." (Gen. 17:19)*

*Let those who desire my vindication shout for joy and be glad, and say evermore, "Great is
the Lord, who delights in the welfare of his servant!" (Ps. 35:27)*

*Where is the wise man? Where is the scribe? Where is the debater of this age? Has not God
made foolish the wisdom of the world? . . . For the foolishness of God is wiser than men,
and the weakness of God is stronger than men. . . . but God chose what is foolish in the
world to shame the wise, God chose what is weak in the world to shame the strong, . . . We
are fools for Christ's sake, but you are wise in Christ. We are weak, but you are strong.
You are held in honor, but we in disrepute. (1Cor. 1:20, 25, 27 and 4:10)*

FUNNY THING ABOUT DYING

Recently some friends of mine recalled an incident that happened in
their family more than twenty-five years ago. The wife's maternal
grandmother had died, aged ninety-five. The wife was very pregnant
with their third child. The grandmother's passing prompted a mixed array
of feelings amongst the family members, as such occasions typically do.
Apart from the grief and sadness associated with her death, there were
some lingering tensions associated with her life.

My friends travelled to the town where the funeral was to be held.
They stayed in the family house, the front of which had a cement slab
verandah, with no rails, stairs in the middle and a drop of three to four
feet all the way around. As they were leaving for the funeral, my friends'
seven-year-old son—a particularly bright young lad whom we shall call
Simon—was absorbed in a book. Simon wandered out the front door, still
reading his book, crossed the verandah, missed the stairs completely and
fell in a muddy puddle.

His mother recalls taking him inside, sitting him on a chair and
pulling his pants off to clean them. Whilst she sponged his pants, Simon
sat on the chair, in jacket, tie and underpants, still absorbed in the book.
We all laughed heartily at this story attached to the grandmother's funeral.

The event is a little slice of life, so typical of what happens. Why would we laugh? Surely when one is going to a funeral, one should maintain greater decorum and respect? On the other hand, maybe the occurence of comedy in the shadow of tragedy is no coincidence?

Consider the following examples from a group of insightful obervers of the human condition:

1. Evelyn Waugh's 1948 novel about death and funerals in Los Angeles.[1] The pages are peopled with comical characters like Dennis Barlow who works at Happier Hunting Grounds, a cemetery for pets, and sends annual memorial cards like "Your little Arthur is thinking of you in heaven today and wagging his tail";[2] Sir Francis Hinsley, the dotty old English knight of the realm, "counterpart of numberless fellow-countrymen exiled in the barbarous regions of the world," who unceremoniously kills himself, "strung to the rafters";[3] Aimee Thanatogenos the "Mortuary Hostess" at Whispering Glades necropolis, confused in love, kills herself with an injection of embalming fluid; Mr Joyboy, a mortician who is capable of massaging the most contorted face of a corpse into something acceptable, helps Dennis to incinerate Aimee in one of the pet ovens at Happier Hunting Grounds.

2. Woody Allen's films and plays. They repeatedly ask the big questions about life and death, meaning and purpose, whether God exists. Even as the audience or reader is plunged into these metaphysical probings, they find themselves laughing uproariously. For example, one cannot help laughing when Allen describes an attempted suicide "by wetting my nose and inserting it in a light socket. Unfortunately there was a short in the wiring, and I merely caromed off the ice box."[4] In *Zelig* the chameleon character of that name is told by a doctor that he has a tumor and may die in a few weeks. The doctor dies instead. In *Love and Death* the two main characters, Sonia and Boris, discuss the meaning of life in a piece that is vintage Allen: "*Boris:* What if there is no God? . . . What if we are just a bunch of absurd people running around with no rhyme or reason? *Sonia:* But if there is no God, then life has no meaning. Why go on living? Why not just commit suicide? *Boris:* Well, let's not get hysterical! I could be wrong. I'd hate to blow my brains out then read in the papers they found something."

3. Monty Python's *The Meaning of Life*. The film opens with a conversation between half a dozen fish in a tank at a restaurant. The fish have the faces of the Monty Python crew. After they have all bid each other good morning the third fish (Terry Gilliam) calls out, "Hey,

look. Howard's being eaten." The waiter serves a grilled fish to a large man. The second fish (John Cleese) says, "Makes you think, doesn't it?" The fourth fish (Eric Idle) joins in, "I mean . . . what's it all about?" The fifth fish (Terry Jones) says "Beats me" and the film begins. It ends with a group of yuppies at a dinner party being visited by the Grim Reaper—they have eaten salmon with botulism. In between, Monty Python fans shriek with laughter at one absurd and/or grotesque scene after another.

WHAT IS COMEDY?

It would obviously be untrue to say that we find death comical. Psychopaths might find it amusing, normal people usually do not. It would be equally untrue to claim that comedy in the shadow of literal death is the only kind of comedy.[5] But it may not be untrue to say that the kind of comedy indicated above is, in some sense, paradigmatic. That is, it contains a foundational pattern that is universal to the human experience of comedy.

Marshal McLuhan said somewhere that we joke about the things that grieve us. And from the Bible writers to contemporary psychologists, one message comes across clearly: Truth grieves us. "Human kind cannot bear too much reality," said T. S. Eliot.[6] George Bernard Shaw observed that his way of joking is to tell the truth—it's the funniest joke in the world.

Comedy is about the incongruous, the absurd and the ridiculous. Those moments when the truth—truth that otherwise would worry the living daylights out of us—is exposed in safety. We poke fun at it, whistle past the graveyard of life. When the Monty Python troop has three London accountants, walking along like a thousand of their kind, replete with bowler hats and umbrellas, suddenly turn and dive into the harbour, we laugh. We laugh for the same reason we laugh when the fat lady slips on the banana skin or the man in a tuxedo has a pie thrown in his face at a fancy party. The masks are lifted and the social pretenses are laid bare— those "vital lies" that reassure us that everything really is just fine.[7] What can we do but laugh?[8]

There is something terribly ridiculous about our lives. Soren Kierkegaard speaks of the human being as like two horses hitched to a carriage—the one is Pegasus of ancient mythology, the winged horse that would fly, the other is an old earthbound nag that just plods along. We are a metaphysical absurdity—made to be companions of God, to be united with God . . . yet . . . "gods who shit," as Ernest Becker has said. Thomas Merton writes well of this when he discusses the vocation of the hermit and some of the realities of solitude:

> Nor do I promise to cheer anybody up with optimistic answers to all the sordid difficulties and uncertainties which attend the life of interior solitude. Perhaps in the course of these reflections, some of the difficulties will be mentioned. The first of them has to be taken note of from the very start: the disconcerting task of facing and accepting one's own absurdity. The anguish of realising that underneath the apparently logical pattern of a more or less "well organized" and rational life, there lies an abyss of irrationality, confusion, pointlessness, and indeed of apparent chaos. This is what immediately impresses itself upon the man who has renounced diversion. It cannot be otherwise: for in renouncing diversion, he renounces the seemingly harmless pleasure of building a tight, self-contained illusion about himself and about his little world. He accepts the difficulty of facing the million things in his life which are incomprehensible, instead of simply ignoring them. Incidentally, it is only when the apparent absurdity of life is faced in all truth that faith really becomes possible. Otherwise, faith tends to be a kind of diversion, a spiritual amusement, in which one gathers up accepted, conventional formulas and arranges them in the approved mental patterns, without bothering to investigate their meaning, or asking whether they have any practical consequences in one's life.[9]

Comedy is a most subtle thing in human existence. When we speak of comedy as a display of the incongruous and absurd in life we presume it is something different from moral irresponsibility or sheer silliness. We hardly think it comedy when elected officials mishandle the State's finances, when parents abuse their children, when the immature engage in dangerous tomfoolery. Though any of these might give rise to comedy. We speak of "black humour" when we make jokes about otherwise very painful, sickening or simply terrifying situations. Comedy also depends on who speaks, when it is said, how it is said and so on. Not everyone would evoke laughter, for example, if they said and did what Woody Allen says and does.[10]

We have all been present when an attempt is made to be funny and it falls flat—the timing was wrong, it was inappropriate for the company, the teller was simply not a funny person. It is like jumping onto what looks like solid ground and it turns out to be a thin layer of moss covering a deep well. You disappear into the dark waters beneath the moss.

Comedy is never far from tragedy, laughter from tears, good humor from insensitivity, pointing to the absurd and incongruous from being simply vulgar.[11] Perhaps the best comedians are those with the deepest sense of tragedy? Perhaps we never get beyond mere insensitivity, vulgarity and superficiality unless we have submitted to the tragic? Life may remain tragically trivial and devoid of real comedy, despite our laughter, until we know ourselves as participants in a tragedy.

COMEDY AND THE CHRISTIAN TRADITION

In his bestselling novel, *The Name of the Rose*, Italian writer Umberto Eco fashions a wonderful story of mystery and intrigue around one man's efforts to prevent a treatise on laughter by Aristotle from becoming available for general consumption. The setting is a monastery in early fourteenth century Europe. The protagonist, Father Jorge, is willing to kill in order to prevent this treatise falling into the "wrong" hands. He is a humorless man who is also blind. Jorge expresses his rigid views on orthodoxy to the English monk-sleuth, William of Baskerville. William asks Jorge "What frightened you in this discussion of laughter?" and Jorge replies:

> Laughter is weakness, corruption, the foolishness of our flesh. Laughter remains base, a defense for the simple, a mystery desecrated for the plebeians. But here, here—now Jorge struck the table with is finger, near the book William was holding open—there the function of laughter is reversed, it is elevated to art, the doors of the world of the learned are opened to it, it becomes the object of philosophy, and of perfidious theology.[12]

Eco has touched a raw nerve! It is not that comedy and laughter have been lacking from our lives as such. Rather, there is in Christian teaching and practice—in all the denominations—a tendency to emphasize the tragic view of life and thus fail to appreciate the comedy. The Jesuit author Thomas Clancy highlights this well in reference to the advice of a Jesuit Superior General:

> Whatever is pleasing is to be avoided for the precise reason that it is pleasing. Whatever is displeasing is to be sought for the precise reason that it is displeasing, unless some just motive persuades otherwise, or rather some just *and certain* motive of the divine service and glory *commands* otherwise.[13]

This is not unlike the mood of *The Imitation of Christ* by Thomas à Kempis, a favorite text of Catholics and Protestants alike.[14] St Ignatius of Loyola counsels the exercitant against laughter in the early part of the Spiritual Exercises.[15] St Benedict wrote in his rule that the monks were not to laugh.[16]

Yet Meister Eckhart wrote a sermon on the laughter of God.[17] What are we to make of this? If we are right in our earlier claim that Biblical revelation does not *impose* but *expose*, that the Real is laid bare by the person and teaching of Jesus, there must be comedy in the Bible, at least implicitly, or we must be deceived in thinking there is comedy in life. Maybe those dour, puritanical wowsers are right—do we need to wake up to ourselves and realize that there is no real comedy in life for those who see the truth, there is only tragedy?

Once again we see how subtle comedy is. While laughter is the normally accepted expression of the appreciation of comedy and humor, do we not laugh sometimes when there is no comedy? Laughter can be, as St Ignatius was aware, a distraction. We may laugh when we are anxious, for example. Laughter can be an avoidance mechanism. Perhaps laughter can even be a sign that we have *not* gotten the joke? Furthermore, we may appreciate comedy but not laugh—at least not out loud. As with other issues of life, the appreciation might defy the commonly used ways to express ourselves. Laughter is not the real issue. Comedy is the real issue. Laughter and comedy do not always go together.

The surprising and the unsuspected are the bread and butter of comedy. "The tragic is the inevitable. The comic is the unforseeable."[18] True comedy is the truth sayer. It speaks the truths we are too frightened, timid or ignorant to speak. As we indicated above, the most surprising thing about comedy is that, at its best, it is grounded in an appreciation of the tragic. We do not speak of "comic tragedy." We do speak of "tragi-comedy." Tragedy is never funny. Comedy is always, in the end, pointing us towards tragedy, albeit in a way that softens the blow.

Is it drawing a long bow, for example, to find comedy in the midst of the Passion narrative? Peter's grand protests of fidelity to Jesus, especially since we know the outcome, are both pathetic and comic.[19] Poor old Peter, impetuous, generous, passionate and foolish. You cannot help loving him for his sheer humanity. The young man who is stripped of his linen cloth and hares off into the night terrified with nothing on—and the most solemn and tragic moment of human history is unfolding right under his nose![20] And Malchus, the High Priest's slave has one of his ears separated from his head by Peter in the same incident.[21] The motley crew, half exhilarated, half terrified, half stumbles, half rushes off to the High Priest. Then Pilate presents "the King" to the rabble before crucifying him. The cross bears the sign for all to see: "Jesus of Nazareth King of the Jews." This, we believe, is the story of our salvation—the redemption of the cosmos! Yes, the greatest tragicomedy that has ever been enacted, or ever will be. "I have told you this so that my joy may be in you and that your joy may be complete."[22] Only those who have a deep appreciation of both tragedy and comedy can begin to comprehend this story, the Good News.[23] Can you have faith and not have a good sense of humor?

St Paul's First Letter to the Corinthians intimates something of that comprehension. The Corinthians were a rather wild crowd, at times even quite uncontrollable. Yet Paul has a soft spot for them and speaks from the heart when he lays bare the essence of our faith. Paul is aware that, from a purely human point of view, faith in the resurrection is just a little outlandish:

> Now if Christ is preached as raised from the dead, how can some of you say that there is no resurrection of the dead? But if there is no resurrection of the dead, then Christ has not been raised; if Christ has not been raised, then our preaching is in vain and your faith is in vain. We are even found to be misrepresenting God, because we testified of God that he raised Christ, whom he did not raise if it is true that the dead are not raised. For if the dead are not raised, then Christ has not been raised. If Christ has not been raised, your faith is futile and you are still in your sins. Then those also who have fallen asleep in Christ have perished. If for this life only we have hoped in Christ, we are of all men most to be pitied.[24]

Among the Desert Fathers of the third and fourth centuries we find a deep apprehension of the Real beyond the real, accompanied by an equally deep sense of the ridiculous:

> A brother asked one of the elders, saying: There are two brothers, of whom one remains praying in his cell, fasting six days at a time and doing a great deal of penance. The other one takes care of the sick. Which one's work is more pleasing to God? The elder replied: If that brother who fasts six days at a time were to hang himself up by the nose, he could not equal the one who takes care of the sick.[25]

When Saint Gregory of Nazianzen's brother Caesarius died, their mother wore festive clothes to the funeral. This was in accord with a belief strongly held at that time that the Christian's faith in Jesus the Christ and the resurrection should dominate one's reactions—especially one's reactions to death. The point was not to do away with joy and laughter but to find it in the right place. This is clearly open to misinterpretation, and the subtlety of it has been too often missed. Faith in the last things can very easily become rejection of the present things, love of heaven hatred of earth, hope in things eternal despair in things temporal.

Given the total context of the lives and writings of people like Benedict, Bernard and Ignatius, it is difficult to sustain any argument that they lacked an appreciation for the comedy of life. I believe any genuine monk is someone who has definitely gotten the joke! They, like all the great spiritual guides, cut through the superficial and illusory that occupies so much of our time, energy and talent. The difference between us and them is that they had a much deeper sense of what matters and what does not.

Elie Wiesel is not a comedian, at least not in the sense in which we commonly use that word. Yet I believe it would be wrong to say that he has no sense of the comedy of life. Like anybody who has been forced to live what he has been forced to live, and face the tragic dimension of life like he has faced the tragic dimension of life, the word "comic" is never found on its own—it is always attached to the word "tragic." He sees beyond the separation of the two and knows life as a "tragicomedy." As we read Wiesel's reflections on Isaac, we get the unmistakable impression that he is looking to Isaac as a kindred spirit from whom he can draw some inspiration and encouragment. Wiesel writes:

> Why was the most tragic of our ancestors named Isaac, a name which evokes and signifies laughter? Here is why. As the first survivor, he had to teach us, the future survivors of Jewish history, that it is possible to suffer and despair an entire lifetime and still not give up the art of laughter. Isaac, of course, never freed himself from the traumatizing scenes that violated his youth; the holocaust had marked him and continued to haunt him forever. Yet he remained capable of laughter. And in spite of everything he did laugh.[26]

Our ancestors in the faith, Abraham and Sarah, were called forth by God on a journey to an unknown destination. Ridiculous as it seems, that is everyone's lot. As a sign of his promise to be with Abraham and Sarah God gave them a child—Isaac. The Hebrew word *Isaac* means *God laughs*.

Is it far fetched to think that God has a sense of humor and that his laughter accompanies us too? To know that laughter we must do as Abraham and Sarah did, leave the safety of the pretenses that give us a "home" and go into the desert of the absurd, the incongruous, and the incomprehensible. There we might see the unforseeable—that good humor and good faith are constant and inseparable companions.

PRACTICAL SUGGESTIONS

a) Recall an incident or joke you found particularly amusing. Starting from there, try to formulate your own working definition of what comedy is. See if you can find an example of this in the Gospels.

b) Read one of the novels mentioned in this chapter. *The Loved One* by Evelyn Waugh, *Porterhouse Blue* and *Riotous Assembly* by Tom Sharpe are all short and eminently readable. Umberto Eco's *The Name of the Rose* is a little more daunting but rewards the persistent. Morris West's *Clowns of God* is also worth reading. Heinrich Böll's short stories are also recommended.

c) What could it mean to say "the Lord delights in his people" (cf. Ps. 18:19; 35:27; 44:3)? Can you imagine the Lord "delighting" in you? Meditate on these things.

Notes
1 Evelyn Waugh, *The Loved One: An Anglo-American Tragedy*. Satirists generally have mastered the art of laying bare the dreadful truths of life in a way that exposes the comedy hidden there. Another contemporary author who is brilliant at this is Tom Sharpe. His *Porterhouse Blue* (a satire on higher education) and *Riotous Assembly* (a satire on apartheid) are both extremely funny and insightful.
2 Waugh 1977, p.3f.
3 Op. cit., p.37.
4 Woody Allen 1975, p.4.
5 Clearly there are other styles of comedy. Furthermore, the details of comedy vary between individuals and from culture to culture. What amuses you may not amuse me, and vice versa.
6 T. S. Eliot, "Burnt Norton," 1971 42f.
7 The term "vital lie" is Ernest Becker's. See his *The Denial of Death*, especially Chapter 4. If you want to appreciate something of the deeper significance of comedy, note the difference between being the *observer* as distinct from being the *butt* of the joke.
8 Circus clowns throughout the world have always known of this organic tie between the tragic and the comic. Why is the clown typically portrayed as a sad person? Leoncavallo's Canio in the opera *I Pagliacci* is a powerful portrayal of this phenomenon. The stories of Heinrich Böll often enough capture this same ambivalence. See *The Stories of Heinrich Böll* 1986.
9 Thomas Merton 1960, p.179f. This is reminiscent of Ivan Illich's comment to the effect that faith is getting the joke!

10   For example, in *Love and Death* the two characters have the following exchange: "*Sonia*: The only truly happy person I know is Berdykov, the village idiot. *Boris*: Well, it's easy to be happy, you know, when your one concern in life is finding out how much saliva to dribble." In the film it passes as genuine comedy. Out of context it is simply offensive, not at all funny. The Monty Python film, *The Life of Brian* comes very close to being offensive to both Jews and Christians alike. The court jester in medieval times was immune from punishment for his wisecracks. Though no doubt there were those who, like Rigoletto, miscalculated and their comedy sadly turned tragic on them. It is not uncommon, either, to find comedians who are sad and/or confused people, all too aware of the tragic dimension of life—for example Woody Allen, Spike Milligan, John Cleese and the late Peter Sellers.

11   One author observes: "To succeed, comedy requires tension and edge. Without hints of inner darkness, it deteriorates into situation comedy" (Mary Flanagan, *The New York Times Book Review*, November 28th, 1993, p. 17.)

12   Umberto Eco 1983, p.473f. Earlier in the encounter with Jorge, William quotes for us from a Greek text in the book that Jorge has been protecting with such ferocity: "In the first book we dealt with tragedy and saw how, by arousing pity and fear, it produces catharsis, the purification of those feelings. As we promised, we will now deal with comedy (as well as with satire and mime) and see how, in inspiring the pleasure of the ridiculous, it arrives at the purification of that passion. That such passion is most worthy of consideration we have already said in the book on the soul, inasmuch as—alone among the animals—man is capable of laughter. etc." (p.468) Umberto Eco fabricated the idea of a treatise on laughter by Aristotle in order to give more bite to his parable on the repression of freedom and learning. "William of Baskerville" is reminiscent of Sherlock Holmes. William's friend Adso ("Adson" in French) is a sort of Watson figure. Eco is reported to have used the twelfth century Bernard of Clairvaux—quite inappropiately I believe—as his model for Jorge.

13   Cited by Thomas Clancy 1979, p. 5. Clancy has added the emphasis. This essay examines the role of "desolation" and "consolation" in the spirituality of St Ignatius. It is well worth reading.

14   Thomas à Kempis draws—in some measure at least—on the spirituality of Bernard of Clairvaux. Both Martin Luther and John Calvin had a good deal of respect for Bernard of Clairvaux, "the last of the Fathers."

15   In the Eighth Addition to the Fifth Exercise in the First Week of the Exercises, St Ignatius counsels "not to laugh nor to say a thing provocative of laughter." (Fleming 1978, p.54) Fleming gives a contemporary reading of this counsel: "I do not try to find occasions to laugh, knowing how often laughter can be an attempt to escape the uneasiness of a situation." (p.55)

16   In Chapter Four of the Rule, St Benedict lists some 72 "instruments of good works." Among them we find "Not to love pleasure," (#12) "not to speak idly nor so as to cause mirth" (#53) and "not to love boisterous laughter." (#54) St Benedict 1975, p.52f). St Bernard of Clairvaux, writing in this same tradition, speaks of "light hearted gaiety at the wrong time" in reference to the third step of pride (Bernard of Clairvaux 1985, p.56)

17   Cf. Raymond Blakney, trans. 1941, p.143–5. Eckhart says "God plays and laughs in good deeds." (p.143)

18   Frederick Buechner 1977 p.57. See the essay "The Gospel as Comedy" for an excellent reflection on comedy in the Bible. Buechner sees it inextricably tied to tragedy. Buechner has a gift for speaking of the tragic without becoming morbid or simply pessimistic, and the comic without becoming superficial or simply flippant. The following books by Buechner are worth reading: *Wishful Thinking: A Theological ABC*, Harper, 1973; *The Sacred Journey: A Memoir of Earlier Days*, Harper, 1982; *Now and Then: A Memoir of Vocation*, Harper, 1983; *Whistling in the Dark: An ABC Theologized*, Harper, 1988.

19 Cf. Mt. 26:30ff.
20 Cf. Mk. 14:51f.
21 Cf. Jn. 18:10f.
22 Jn. 15:11 (NIV). It is significant that the late Karl Rahner uses the context of a meditation on "Shrove Tuesday" to provide us with a lovely reflection on humor. Cf. K. Rahner 1964, pp. 49–56.
23 One author captures this paradoxical, tragicomic mood of the Gospels well: ". . . have you thought that He stained Himself, soiled Himself, being not only with men, but Himself a man . . . And it wasn`t that He put on man like a jacket to take off at night, or to bathe . . . But man He was, as man is man, the maker made Himself the made; God was un-Godded by His own hand . . . He was God from before the beginning, and now never to be clean God again. Never again. Alas! . . . Hosanna!" (Prescott 1952 Vol. 2, pp. 510–11.)
24 1Cor. 15:12-19
25 T. Merton 1960, p.60.
26 Weisel 1976, p.97.

10

SAUL AND DAVID, JUDAS AND PETER

Jesus turned and said to Peter, "Get behind me Satan! You are an obstacle in my path, because the way you think is not God's way but man's." (Mt. 16:23–JB)

As Jesus drew near and came in sight of the city he shed tears over it. (Lk. 19:41–JB)

We know that turning everything to their good God co-operates with all those who love him. (Rom. 8:28–JB)

THE BISHOP CONFRONTED BY A STRANGE LIGHT

In his novel, *Les Misérables*, Victor Hugo presents a meticulous and powerful—if at times a little idealized—portrayal of life in early nineteenth century France. It is a social commentary, in which a certain Bishop Myriel plays an essential role. He is, as it were, the seed of redemption in an otherwise brutal and unforgiving world. Hugo takes a good deal of time and effort early in the novel to portray this man. Bishop Myriel dispenses with the trappings of his episcopacy and gives them to the poor. He is a holy man in the best sense of the word. But he must learn his holiness in the stuff of daily living.

There is one particularly poignant scene where the bishop seeks out an old man ("G.-") living on the edge of town. The man, presumed to be an atheist and a former member of the Revolutionary Convention that had, among other things, been responsible for the Reign of Terror in 1793, was dying. After some conversation, during which the bishop is increasingly impressed by the intelligence and honesty of this man, there is a final moment when reality is turned beautifully on its head. Hugo is a consummate master of such moments:

> No longer gazing at the bishop, he summed up his thought in a few quiet words.
>
> "The brutalities of progress are called revolutions. When they are over we realize this: that the human race has been roughly handled, but that it has advanced."
>
> He did not know, the man of the people, that one by one he had

broken down the bishop's defences. But a last one remained, and from this supreme stronghold Monseigneur Bienvenu (i.e. Bishop Myriel) uttered words scarcely less harsh than those with which the interview had begun.

"Progress must believe in God. The good cannot be served by impiety. An atheist is an evil leader of the human race."

The old man did not answer. A tremor shook him. He looked up at the sky and a tear formed slowly in his eye, to brim over and roll down his pale cheek. Still gazing upward and almost stammering, he murmured to himself:

"Thou who art Perfection! Thou who alone exist."

The bishop was inexpressibly moved.

After a pause the old man pointed to the sky and said: "The infinite has being. It is there. If infinity had no self then self would not be. But it is. Therefore it has a self. The self of infinity is God."

He had spoken those last words in a clear voice and with a quiver of ecstasy, as though he saw some living presence. Then he closed his eyes. The effort had exhausted him. It was plain that in the course of a moment he had lived the few hours that remained to him. His last utterance had brought him very near to death.

The bishop saw that there was no time to lose. He had come there as a priest. His mood of extreme aloofness had changed by degrees to one of deep emotion. Gazing at the closed eyes and taking the old, cold, wrinkled hand in his, he leaned towards the dying man.

"This hour belongs to God," he said. " Do you not think it would be sad if we should have met in vain?"

The old man opened his eyes. There was a shadowed gravity upon his face.

"My lord bishop," he said, speaking with a slowness that was perhaps due more to the dignity of the spirit than to failing strength, "I have passed my life in meditation, study, and contemplation. I was sixty when my country summoned me to take part in her affairs. I obeyed the summons. There were abuses and I fought against them, tyrannies and I destroyed them, rights and principles and I asserted them. Our country was invaded and I defended it; France was threatened and I offered her my life. I was never rich; now I am poor. I was among the masters of the State, and the Treasury vaults were so filled with wealth that we had to buttress the walls lest they collapse under the weight of gold and silver; but I dined in Poverty Street at twenty-two sous a head. I succoured the oppressed and consoled the suffering. I tore up the altar-cloths, it is true; but it was to bind our country's wounds. I have always striven for the advance of mankind towards the light, and sometimes I have resisted progress that was without mercy. I have on occasion protected my rightful adversaries, your fellow-priests. At Peteghem in Flanders, on the spot where the Merovingian kings once had their summer palace, there is an Urbanist convent, the Abbaye de Sainte-Claire en Beaulieu, which I saved from destruction in 1793. I have done my duty, and what good I could, so far as was in my power. And I have been hounded and persecuted, mocked and defamed, cursed and proscribed. I have long known that many people believe they have the right to despise me, and that for the ignorant crowd I wear the face of the damned. I have accepted the isolation of hatred, hating no one. Now at the age of eighty-six I am on the point of death. What do you ask of me?"

"Your blessing," said the bishop, and fell on his knees.

When at length the bishop raised his head there was a look of grandeur on the old man's face. He had died.[1]

Who is "good"? What is "good"? We are perhaps too prone to take our criteria for answering these questions from social custom rather than the One who is good, the One who transcends any human measurement. There is some value in pursuing the answer to these questions by returning to the healing and revealing Word. What do we find there in the events of salvation history?

Events[2] are the primary locus of revelation in the sacred Scriptures. The primary events are the Exodus—with its particular Covenant in the OT—and the Passover or New Exodus—with its particular Covenant in the NT. At the heart of every event the Mystery is revealed in some way. Words give us access, albeit limited, to the revealing event.[3]

People are integral to these biblical events and thus become part of the revealing. To reflect on what happens to these individuals and—perhaps more particularly—how they respond, can be a most revealing process indeed.

In this and the following section, we will look at five individuals and see where they take us. First of all, we will take personalities in contrast—Saul and David, Judas and Peter—and allow the dynamics of this tension to reveal what it will. Secondly we will take one particularly symbolic personality—Mary, the mother of Jesus—and allow the personal symbolism there to address us and form and inform us concerning what is "good."

SAUL AND DAVID: MISTRUST VERSUS TRUST

> Among the men of Benjamin there was a man named Kish . . . He had
> a son named Saul, a handsome man in the prime of life. Of all the
> Israelites there was no one more handsome than he; he stood head and
> shoulders taller than the rest of the people.[4]

Despite his obvious talents as a leader, there is a profound ambivalence
from the very beginning of Saul's reign as king. Although he is chosen by
God and anointed by Samuel,[5] and places himself within the ongoing
history of the Covenant,[6] Saul's very designation as "king" defies the
vocation of Israel.[7] Israel is not like any other nation, it has only one
"king"—the Lord of the Exodus.

   This ambivalence begins to show itself immediately, as Saul usurps
the priestly role of Samuel.[8] Later he is actually to command the massacre
of the priests.[9] Although Saul's reign as king is in fact a militarily
successful one,[10] he is rejected by the Lord because he lacks the obedience
of the true servant.[11] Cut off from the source of redeeming love in the
Mystery, Saul is left to his own increasingly conflicting resources and
slowly disintegrates under their weight.[12] Finally, there is something brave
yet pathetic about his death.[13]

   Saul is a tragic figure. A man of considerable talent, nagged by a stiff-
necked people and troubled by the apparent insecurity of Israel amongst
the other nations, he moves to provide solutions out of his own resources.
This is natural enough, and even commendable. At the merely superficial
level (for instance in military conquests) he is "successful." But he has
moved beyond the realm of the Covenant relationship and its morality.
Saul believes too much in his own abilities and too little in the promise:
"I am with you." Religion is reduced from relationship to ritual and thus
loses its essential quality of being rooted in God's mercy and compassion.
Dislocated from this lifegiving source, Saul's life moves inexorably in the
direction of increased willful striving and despair.

   Deep down *Saul does not trust the Mystery and the promises made.* He
therefore cannot live in openness to that Mystery—he is fundamentally
a disobedient man. Demetrius Dumm writes:

> The sinfulness that distrusts life is illustrated by the tragic life of King
> Saul. He found evil and darkness in his life, as all do, but he allowed
> it to gain the upper hand and to cast a blight eventually on everything
> he did. This is usually a gradual process. It begins with a tendency to

be critical and judgmental which becomes ever more pervasive until it darkens everything. Nothing is beyond criticism; everything is flawed. The final stage in this process is bitterness which drives all enjoyment out of life and makes happy surprises impossible.[14]

Because of the infidelity of Saul, Samuel is sent by the Lord to anoint a new king who will be a faithful servant. He is sent to "Jesse of Bethlehem"[15] to anoint Jesse's son—"the youngest . . . a boy of fresh complexion with fine eyes and pleasant bearing."[16] Paradoxically, this newly anointed one becomes Saul's solace in his misery[17] and "Saul loved him greatly."[18]

   Given Saul's attitude to life, with his radical mistrust contaminating all his thoughts and actions, his unerring ability to turn promise into threat, possibility into impossibility, it was probably predictable that David, his one source of comfort, would soon become his primary source of distress. David's fighting prowess becomes legendary.[19] Saul's anger is aroused and he "turned a jealous eye on David from that day forward."[20] Saul even tries to murder David at the very time he is playing the harp to soothe his anguished spirit.[21] It is typical of people like Saul to bite the hand that feeds them.

   Saul's son Jonathan "made a pact with David to love him as his own soul."[22] David is protected by Jonathan[23] and, having escaped the immediate threat of Saul, he bcomes a wanderer like his ancestors.[24]

   David is hunted by Saul;[25] he has an opportunity to kill Saul but spares him;[26] he eats the consecrated bread;[27] he marries Abigail[28] and Ahinoam,[29] having previously also married Saul's daughter Michal;[30] he joins the Philistines for a time;[31] he is profoundly saddened when he hears of the death of Saul;[32] he becomes King of Judah and Saul's son Ishbaal king of Israel;[33] eventually David becomes King of Israel too;[34] he takes other concubines and wives;[35] he attempts to build a special house for the Lord but is reminded of the true Covenantal relationship between the Lord and the people;[36] his reign is marked by wars and family intrigues;[37] he sins grievously by taking Bathsheeba, Uriah's wife, arranging for the death of Uriah;[38] David repents of his sin and his child, borne by Bathsheeba, dies;[39] he becomes a fugitive in his own kingdom;[40] he mourns the death of the traitor Absalom;[41] he takes a census of the kingdom;[42] he dies and leaves the kingship to Solomon, the son conceived by Bathsheeba when he was consoling her for the death of their first son, born out of the adulterous union.[43]

David is a figure of Israel—and in that, a figure of the whole human family and each one of us. He is an extraordinarily complex mixture of virtue and sin, innocence and pragmatism, a scoundrel and a saint. Beneath it all, however, is *a profound trust in the Lord of the Covenant*. His very sins are occasions for the mercy and compassion of the Lord, revealed in the Covenant, to shine forth. Just as Saul's very virtues occasioned his dislocation from the Covenant, David's very brokenness as a human being occasions his going into that Covenant in depth. Saul's world is limited by his virtues and sins and thus full of impossibilities, David's world—the world of the Real beyond the real—is limitless and full of possibilities. He never becomes lost in the darkness of human affairs because he is deeply rooted in the light of God's mercy and never-ending love for the people. He is always, in the final analysis, open to the Mystery. David is *an obedient man*. Demetrius Dumm writes:

> David's significance is highlighted against the background of Saul. For David was as self-confident and decisive as Saul was insecure and wavering. David had no liturgical scruples when he and his men took and ate the sacred bread (1Sam 21:3–6). David also committed really serious sins, notably when he ordered the death of Uriah to cover up his sin with Bathsheba (2Sam 11). But he was able to repent and seemed to be even better for the experience. Saul managed to turn peccadillos into unforgivable sins; David turned grievous sins into opportunities for grace and growth. Saul was snake-bitten, always in the wrong line of traffic, forever snatching defeat from the jaws of victory! David, by contrast, had a golden touch, won out against all odds, always seemed to know exactly the right thing to say or do.
>
> At first sight it seems that David was lucky and Saul was cursed. But David knew adversity too: the incest against Tamar, the murder of Amnon, the treason of Absalom, the disobedience of Joab. The difference goes much deeper than chance. It is a matter of faith. Saul and David both believed in God and the goodness of God. But Saul, unlike David, seemed incapable of believing in the goodness of God's world, of God's future and of Saul himself. And so he was a worried, anxious man and was always prepared for evil and always found it. David was confident, optimistic, positive; he was prepared for good, for happy surprise and, since God's world is basically good, he was able to find blessing, in spite of problems and setbacks. Saul could not lead Israel, as Samuel sensed, because no one will follow a loser. David was an extraordinary leader because he was ready to see the promise in

others and trusted his own instincts in bringing that promise to fruition.[44]

JUDAS AND PETER: PRAGMATISM VERSUS FAITH

Whatever interpretation we might like to put on Judas' actions, the biblical authors clearly see him as a traitor.[45] He must have had some organizational ability because he was put "in charge of the common fund."[46] He is quick to calculate the "value" of the ointment used by Mary to anoint Jesus.[47] Perhaps Oscar Wilde's description of the cynic as one who knows the cost of everything but the value of nothing fits this man. The boundaries of his imagination and mind—indeed of his whole life— seem to be those set by pragmatic principles. It is not difficult to imagine that Judas had no intention of seeing Jesus crucified when he betrayed him for the thirty pieces of silver. Judas is *a pragmatist* and the pragmatist in him would have already seen Jesus' remarkable facility in getting out of tight spots. What he did not reckon on was the fact that he and Jesus lived in two very different worlds—Jesus' world is the world of the Real beyond the real, a world only accessed by faith, whilst Judas' world is the world of superficial realities, a world easily accessed, and manipulated, by anyone with a bit of talent and cunning.

When finally confronted by the pathetic limitations of his world, Judas despairs. He knows no other possibilities. His pusillanimous view of life does not embrace the limitless possibilities of the Lord of the Covenant. When pushed to the wall, there is no room for mercy and compassion in Judas' world. Thus, the very experience that might have been a blessed turning point, a moment of hitherto undreamt of possibilities, becomes an accursed moment, a moment of predictable impossibility. Judas embodies the tragic irony of the pragmatist: When it comes to the ultimate issues of life, pragmatism is supremely impractical.

Had he remembered Jesus' account of his own temptations in the wilderness—"Man does not live on bread alone"[48]—Judas may have, at this time of cruel testing, been able to enter that world of the Real. We lost a good man!

Peter stands in contrast to Judas. To the outside observer, there may have been little to distinguish Peter and Judas up until the time of the crucifixion. Neither seems to have been aware of what was going on.[49] Both seem, in their own ways, more or less supportive of Jesus. Peter does seem to have leadership potential that Jesus recognizes.[50] And he is a man of *faith*—not the gift of faith to know Jesus as Lord so much as the gift of faith to know life as a promise not a threat.

The crucial difference between the two personalities is seen in the way they handle the confrontation with their own sinfulness. Peter betrays Jesus just as surely as Judas did.[51] But, whereas Judas reacted in a practical way, taking the money back and trying to reverse what he had done,[52] Peter simply "went outside and wept bitterly."[53] He knows there is no human answer to this mystery of evil that is so painfully evident in him. It is not a problem that can be solved by this or that course of action. It is a mystery that can only be lived with when one is rooted in the deep consciousness of the Lord who saves. Only God's mercy can redeem humanity in its misery.

Paradoxically, therefore, Peter's sin is the most blessed moment of his life. At last he can begin to see what Jesus' existence means! His natural appreciation for the mystery of life begins to blossom into a graced appreciation for the Mystery that is Life.

JEAN VALJEAN AND JAVERT: DAVID AND SAUL MEET AGAIN

In Victor Hugo's novel, *Les Misérables*, we find two particularly symbolic characters. Jean Valjean is a man who has been cruelly imprisoned and maltreated in the galleys for some nineteen years. It is little wonder that, after such a period of brutalizing treatment, his outlook on the world is angry and confused. He is given hospitality by the kindly Bishop Myriel whose spirit of compassion and generosity provokes a profound transformation in Valjean. He spends the rest of his life, under assumed names, endeavoring to live by this same spirit. Yet, as an ex-prisoner, he is constantly under threat of suspicion and arrest.

Javert is the police chief dedicated to law and order—and to crushing Valjean. Born in prison, he has grown up in a harsh world. He gives no mercy and expects none. Total and unremitting justice is his concern. However, it is this onesided and distorted sense of justice that brings him into the orbit of Valjean's world of mercy and forgiveness. The experience places Javert in a crisis where he has the possibility of redemption or annihilation. He must choose:

> He could no longer live by his lifelong principles, he had entered a new strange world of humanity, mercy, gratitude and justice other than that

of the law. He contemplated with horror the rising of a new sun—an owl required to see with eagle's eyes. He was forced to admit that kindness existed. The felon had been kind, and, a thing unheard of, so had he. Therefore he had failed himself. He felt himself to be a coward. Javert's ideal was to be more than human; to be above reproach. And he had failed.[54]

There is the tragic irony again. When we bring artificial closure on life and block out the Mystery by idolizing part of life, absolutizing the relative, we end by destroying that which we claim to be so important. Thus, in the end, the pragmatist is impractical, the rationalist irrational and the one obsessed with justice unjust.

This "new strange world" which had been opened up for Valjean by his contact with the bishop, and was now opening up for Javert by his contact with Valjean, is too much for Javert to bear. Rather than enter that world, which meant relinquishing the security of his world of clearcut law and order, he commits suicide.

"The pupil dilates in darkness and in the end finds light, just as the soul dilates in misfortune and in the end finds God."[55] Whilst this was beautifully true of Jean Valjean, it was sadly untrue of Javert. Javert pursued the willful belief that "misfortune" is overcome by duty and strict adherence to laws. He would not allow himself to enter the "misfortune" of his life and thus missed his life altogether.[56]

PRACTICAL INSIGHTS ARISING

Ronald Knox comments in his discussion of the early Montanist heresy:

> The history of Montanism is not to be read as that of a great spiritual revival, maligned by its enemies. It is that of a naked fanaticism, which tried to stampede the Church into greater severity, when she had not forgotten how to be severe. And its chief importance for our present subject is that it helped her to make up her mind, thus early in her experience, about the recurrent problem of human weakness and her own commission to forgive.[57]

The heresy of Montanism began in the latter part of the second century and found the lawyer Tertullian (c.155–222) as its most articulate disciple. Later, in the fourth century the Donatist movement—named after a certain Bishop Donatus—was to raise a similar challenge for the Church. The Donatists taught that sacraments enacted by those priests who had denied their faith under persecution ("traditores"—"traitors") were not valid. This view, which implies, by extension, that the validity of the sacraments depends upon the fidelity of the minister rather than God acting through the Church, was condemned by a Council in Rome in 314. However it persisted long after that, as is evidenced by the fact that St Augustine was still fighting it a century later. (Perhaps it is a heresy re-emerging in our own time?)

Various religious renewals and revivals down through the centuries have slipped into similar heretical stances. It is one thing to call the people back to fidelity to the Covenant—as the prophets of old did so relentlessly and as Jesus Himself did—it is quite another to impose a rigid regimen of "holiness" that lacks the primary characteristics of that Covenant: faith in God's mercy and compassion.

There are at least three lessons we can draw from the foregoing. In the first place the Mystery revealed in the Covenants is the beginning, the end and the context for Christian life formation and any reflection on it. In the second place there is a "mystery of evil" that affects the very roots of human existence and cannot be overcome by human effort alone. In the third place it is in our experience of that "mystery of evil" in our own lives that we are most likely to know the Mystery in its mercy and compassion, faithful from generation to generation.

Human existence only finds its fulfillment in God. If I am holy it is ultimately because of God's mercy. "God's mercy is our merit" (St Bernard of Clairvaux). If I am genuinely fulfilled as a human being it is because of God's mercy.

The mystery of evil is a reality. The fact that we do not seem to have an adequate mythology to speak about that mystery is a decided disadvantage. It may even promote the illusion that evil is a human creation and can be overcome by trying harder or by setting up better religious, social, economic and political structures. We must always struggle for such structures, but without denying or being immobilized by the truth that "Sin" is in the world and can ultimately be overcome only by Christis.[58] Naive and un-Christian optimism about the essential goodness of people—just as surely as naive and un-Christian pessimism about the inherent evil of people—tends to destroy the vigilance and discipline that allows us to co-operate hopefully and effectively with the grace of the Spirit in fighting for the Kingdom of Light.

But there is even more to it than this. The classics of the tradition, building on the life and teachings of Jesus himself, warn us time and again:

It is only by coming face to face with my own misery, humbly acknowledging it and laying myself bare before the Lord that I ever know His mercy. *It is precisely in the experience of our need for salvation that we know him who saves.* If my fallenness—misery, sinfulness . . . call it what you will—is but a theoretical notion to me, so too will my knowledge of Jesus the Christ be but a theoretical notion. It seems that until human beings come face to face with the uncontrollable within themselves—the chaos and despair that haunt us all and typically only come into view when our taken for granted worlds are disrupted—they are not likely to recognize their absolute need for God. And even then the illusions of mastery and control, sometimes canonized by the rhetoric of Christian asceticism, tend to persist.

Adrian Van Kaam offers a balanced perspective when he writes:

The Lord will never ask how successful we were in overcoming a particular vice, sin or imperfection. He will ask us, "Did you humbly and patiently accept this mystery of iniquity in your life? How did you deal with it? Did you learn from it to be patient and humble? Did it teach you to trust not your own ability but my love? Did it enable you to understand better the mystery of iniquity in the lives of others? Did it give you the most typical characteristic of the truly religious person—that he never judges or condemns the sin or imperfection in others?" The religious man knows from his own life that the demon of evil can be stronger than man even despite his best attempts; he knows that it is the patience, humility and charity learned from this experience that count. Success and failure are accidental. The joy of the Christian is never based on his personal religious success but on the knowledge that his Redeemer lives. The Christian is the one who is constantly aware of his need of salvation. Acceptance of the mystery of iniquity in our project of existence is a school of mildness, mercy, forgiveness and loving understanding of our neighbor.[59]

PRACTICAL SUGGESTIONS

(a) Ask the question of yourself: *Is there anything I can imagine myself doing that God could not or would not forgive?* Use Gendlin's focusing technique and perhaps your journal to listen attentively to the feeling response this question evokes within you. Conclude with a brief prayer before God.

(b) Ask the question of yourself: *Is there anything/anyone which/who remains to be forgiven by you?* The "anyone" might be yourself. Again, use

Gendlin's focusing technique and perhaps your journal to listen attentively to the feeling response this question evokes. Do not try willfully to forgive. Wait upon the grace of the moment. Discover the bondage that is still preventing you from being free. Remember, your unwillingness to forgive "them" is *your* bondage, not theirs. Remember also that forgiveness is a grace for which we can only dispose ourselves. Then we wait. Conclude with a prayer for God's blessing for "them," commend yourself into the merciful hands of God. Stay with the God of mercy for a time.

(c) Designate a period—say one month—during which time you say the following prayer of St Ignatius as fervently as you can:

Take O Lord and receive my entire liberty, my memory, my understanding, my whole will. All that I am and all that I possess you have given me. I surrender it all to you to be disposed of according to your most holy will. Give me only your love and your grace, with these I will be rich enough and desire nothing more.

(d) Pay gentle attention to your reactions to other people. Next time you find yourself passing judgment in an angry or negative way, pause and ask yourself what is happening. It may be that you have experienced or witnessed an injustice which gives rise to an appropriate anger. It may also be that there is another agenda operating. Listen carefully to your feelings. You might find it helpful to use the focusing technique of Eugene Gendlin and your journal. (Note: Those moments when we "catch" ourselves doing/saying/experiencing life in a certain way are often the most revealing and potentially the most healing and growthful. We "catch" ourselves before the defenses can swing into action and obfuscate the issue!)

Notes

1 V. Hugo 1987, p.57f.
2 From the Latin e and *venire*—*to come out*. Events are those occasions where the Real comes out or shines forth in an extraordinary way. Events are epiphanies, from the Greek *phaino*, meaning *to show*. Our English word *phenomenon* has the same roots and implied meaning.
3 G. E. Wright observes that the Bible is not primarily the word of God but the account of God's actions (1952, p.107).
4 1Sam. 9:1–2; cf. also 10:23–4.
5 Cf. 1Sam. 9:15.
6 Cf. 1Sam. 12:6ff.
7 Cf. 1Sam. 8:1–9.
8 Cf. 1Sam. 13:8ff.
9 Cf. 1Sam. 22:6–23.

10 Cf. 1Sam. 14:47–8.
11 Cf. 1Sam. 15:10–23.
12 Cf.1Sam. 16:14–16; 18:10–11; 28:3ff.
13 Cf. 1Sam. 31:1–13.
14 Dumm 1987, p.52.
15 1Sam. 16:1.
16 1Sam. 16:11–12.
17 Cf. 1Sam. 16:19–23.
18 Ibid.
19 Cf. 1Sam. 18:6–7 and 29:5.
20 1Sam. 18:9.
21 1Sam. 18:10–11 and 19:8ff.
22 1Sam. 18:3.
23 1Sam. 19:1–3 and 20:1–21:1.
24 1Sam. 22:1ff.
25 1Sam. 23:19ff.
26 1Sam. 24:1ff.
27 1Sam. 21:2–10.
28 1Sam. 25:40.
29 1Sam. 25:43.
30 1Sam. 18:20–7.
31 1Sam. 27:5–12.
32 2Sam. 1:1–27.
33 2Sam. 8–11.
34 2Sam. 5:1–5.
35 2Sam. 5:13–16.
36 2Sam. 7:1–29.
37 2Sam. 8:1–9:13.
38 2Sam. 11:1–27.
39 2Sam. 12:1–25.
40 2Sam. 15:13ff.
41 2Sam. 19:1–9.
42 2Sam. 24:1–9.
43 1Kings 2:1–11.
44 Dumm 1987, pp.41–2.
45 Cf.Mt. 10:4.
46 Jn. 13:29.
47 Cf. Jn. 12:5.
48 Mt. 4:1–11.
49 For example, Jesus' rebuke to Peter (Mt. 16:21–3) immediately after Peter's bold profession of faith (Mt. 16:13:20).
50 Cf. Mt. 16:18.
51 Cf. Lk. 22:55ff; Mk. 14:66ff.; Mt. 26:69ff.
52 Cf. Mt. 27:3ff.
53 Lk. 22:62.
54 Hugo 1987, p.1106.
55 Op. cit., p.1078.
56 See Henry James, *The Beast in the Jungle* for the exploration of a similar theme.
57 Knox 1962, p.49.
58 Cf. Rom. 5:12ff.
59 A. Van Kaam 1980, 14f. Suggested further reading: Graham Greene's *The Power and the Glory* and *A Burnt Out Case*; Flannery O'Connor's "The Lame Shall Enter First" and "Revelation"; Shusaku Endo's *Silence*; Walker Percy's *Love in the Ruins* and *The*

Second Coming; Michael Mott's The Seven Mountains of Thomas Merton; Emma Pierce's Ordinary Insanity and Passion for the Possible; Harriet Doerr's Stones for Ibarra; Joseph H. Berke's I Haven't Had To Go Mad Here; Bernard Bro's The Little Way; Guy Gaucher's The Passion of Therese of Lisieux; William Lynch's Images of Hope; Noel Dermott O'Donoghue's Heaven in Ordinarie; Marie Noel's Notes to Myself.

11
MARY THE MOTHER OF JESUS

The angel of Yahweh appeared to (Manoah) and said to her . . . you will conceive and bear a son. (Jg. 13:2–5)

Then Hannah said this prayer: 'My heart exults in Yahweh'. (1Sam. 2:1)

When the appointed time came, God sent his Son, born of a woman. (Gal. 4:5)

A SYMBOLIC FIGURE

In the previous chapter we considered the contrasting figures of David and Saul, Peter and Judas. In this chapter we will look at Mary, the Mother of Jesus, as a symbolic figure in the Christian tradition. In the former instance, we had little of devotional and theological tradition to deal with. In the case of Mary, there is considerable devotional and theological tradition. Some of it is soundly based in sacred Scripture, and is very enlightening. Some, however, is more limited, being strongly influenced by cultural, political and historical factors which have tended to obfuscate the real symbolic value of Mary. Andrew Greeley offers some insights that can help to clear the ground for our reflections.

In his evocative book *The Mary Myth*, Greeley takes up the specifically symbolic approach to Mary. He writes:

> The Marian symbol is surely one of the most powerful symbols in the Western tradition. Virtually every major painter from the fifth to the sixteenth century painted at least one Madonna. Great cathedrals sprang up all over Europe and still stand. Poets sing her praises, including some improbable characters such as Petrarch, Boccaccio, François Villon, Shelley, Byron, Rilke.
> If Enlightenment rationalism is truly moribund—and the signs that it is are overwhelming—then we have entered into an era of open marketplace for religious symbols. . . . Under such circumstances, the Mary symbol ought at least to be reconsidered on the possibility that a symbol that has had so much power for most of the history of the Western world as it did may still have some power of illumination in our time.[1]

Greeley goes on to cite the author Ian Barbour[2] on the role of myth in religion:

> According to Barbour, myths offer ways of ordering experience, inform man about himself, express a saving power in human life, provide patterns for human actions, and are enacted in rituals (pages 21–22). Barbour observes (page 23) "In the Western religions myth is indeed tied primarily to historical events rather than to phenomena in nature. This difference is crucial for conceptions of history, time and ethics, but it need not lead us to deny the presence of myth in the Bible. Divine action is in itself no more directly observable in history than in primordial time or nature."[3]

To approach a reflection on Mary the Mother of Jesus in this mythic framework may help us to avoid some of the silly and occasionally tragic arguments over her. For example, the Protestant Revolt of the sixteenth century and much of the Catholic response:

> The antipathy of some of the reformers and their followers to Mary was a disastrous mistake, as were the Catholic superstitions which in part caused the antipathy and the triumphalism which followed. . . . The reformers were quite correct in insisting that Mary had taken on a quasi divine role in the Catholic tradition. They were wrong, however, in thinking that such a role detracted from the worship of God; for we shall see that Mary, like all feminine deities, reflects a central component of the deity and does not detract from its fullness.[4]

Greeley cites one Protestant author:

> "Ignoring the place of the Blessed Virgin in the Incarnation and the whole process of salvation has given Protestantism a harsh thoroughly masculine emphasis. . . . The absence (of tenderness and affection) in Protestantism has led to an overemphasis on a harsh prophetic picture of God with its attending pre-occupation with judgment. . . . The development of a mature Mariology in Protestant thinking could do much to temper the harsh potrayal of the God of judgment and provide it with a healthy (and, I might add scriptural) concept of God's mercy."[5]

Greeley goes on to indicate the direction of his thesis to be explored in the rest of the book:

> I will contend that Mary is a symbol of the feminine component of the deity. She represents the human insight that the Ultimate is

passionately tender, seductively attractive, irresistably inspiring, and graciously healing. I will argue that the Mary symbol arises out of the human "limitation experience" of sexual differentiation. Mary is, in other words, part of a great tradition of female deities, all of whom reflect the human conviction that God has feminine as well as masculine characteristics, a conviction arising spontaneously and inevitably from the profound, disturbing, and shattering experience of sex differentiation.[6]

The context out of which Greeley writes is explicitly sociological. His written style is racy, and even sensationalist at times. Yet he lays bare some of the crucial human formational issues and possibilities that can assist us in our reflections. Our discussion will presume the theological and exegetical issues that are essential to any total picture of Mary in the Christian tradition. Our concern will center around Mary as a specifically feminine *symbol*, emerging in the Scriptures and significantly complementing our human experience of both human and Christian life formation as sexually differentiated.[7]

THE COVENANT AS INITIAL CONTEXT

We have already noted that in the revelation of the Covenant in the OT, God's enduring mercy and compassion are central to the relationship to be pursued with the chosen people.[8] The Hebrew word *raham* used there is closely tied in its meaning to the word for *womb*—the love expressed is analogous to that of the mother who, having brought forth life from the depths of her bodily being, loves that life from those same depths.

The seventh century prophet Zephaniah implies similar imagery when he renews the promise of messianic salvation for the poor and oppressed people of Israel, "the daughter of Zion":

> Sing aloud, O daughter of Zion; shout O Israel! Rejoice and exult with all your heart, O daughter of Jerusalem! The Lord has taken away the judgments against you, he has cast out your enemies. The King of Israel, the Lord is in your midst; you shall fear evil no more. On that day it shall be said to Jerusalem: 'Do not fear, O Zion; Let not your hands grow weak. The Lord your God is in your midst, a warrior who gives victory; he will rejoice over you with gladness, he will renew you in his love; he will exult over you with loud singing as on a day of festival. "I will remove disaster from you so that you will not bear reproach for it. Behold at that time I will deal with all your oppressors.

And I will save the lame and gather the outcast, and I will change their shame into praise and renown in all the earth. At that time I will bring you home, at the time when I gather you together; yea I will make you renowned and praised among all the peoples of the earth, when I restore your fortunes before your eyes," says the Lord.[9]

This re-affirmation of the spirit of the Covenant, comes at the end of the prophet's writing in which he strongly rebukes the people for allowing the inroads of pagan deities. The Covenant mood, though powerfully obvious in this entire piece quoted, is perhaps best seen in the repeated phrase "in your midst." William Dalton[10] says of this phrase: "Yahweh is in the midst of Zion ('*beqirbeka*'), which could otherwise be translated, '*in your womb.*'"[11] Dalton notes the use of this same ambiguous phraseology in Joel 2:27 ("You will know that I am in the midst of Israel"), Zechariah 2:14 ("Sing, rejoice daughter of Zion, for I am coming to you, to dwell in the middle of you") and Zechariah 9:9 ("Rejoice heart and soul, daughter of Zion, shout with gladness, daughter of Jerusalem. See now your king comes to you"). Dalton goes on to say: "Throughout, the emphasis is on the messianic joy of the daughter of Zion, on the coming of Yahweh as king to her midst (an expression which is the equivalent of "to her womb")."[12]

Interestingly, this perspective draws attention, not to "the womb of God" from which the Covenant life and love is initially seen to spring, but to "the womb of the daughter of Zion"—the womb of the chosen people—to whom that life and love speaks. Without apology and so easily, sacred Scripture uses the language of sexual differentiation to draw our attention to the nature of the Covenant and, by implication, to the stunning destiny of human existence as such.

THE NT PERSPECTIVE OF LUKE[13]

Wilfred Harrington notes that the first two chapters of Luke's Gospel— the so-called "infancy narratives"—are "dominated by the idea of messianic fulfillment."[14] The description of the Annunciation has a distinct literary form, clearly denoting Luke's intention to see in Mary the fulfillment of the Promise.[15] Harrington also notes further:

(In Lk. 1:28) the occurrence, in such a semitically colored narrative, of the Greek formula "chaire" in place of the Semitic "Peace!" is so surprising that one hesitates to accept it at its face value. On closer inspection we find that Luke has a specific OT passage in mind:

Zephaniah 3:14–17 (cf. Joel 2:21–7; Zechariah 9:9f.): "Sing aloud, O daughter of Zion; Rejoice . . . O daughter of Jerusalem!" The word "Rejoice!"—also occurring in Joel and Zechariah and nowhere else in the Septuagint—is "chaire," the same term used by the evangelist. Since that passage of Zephaniah underlies Luke 1:30, "chaire" must have the meaning "Rejoice!"—an invitation to rejoice at the advent of the messianic times.[16]

Mary's subsequent "Magnificat," put on her lips by Luke as she encounters her cousin Elizabeth, is "a catena of OT reminiscences and leans especially on the canticle of Hannah (1Samuel 2:1–10)."[17] Luke is intent on portraying Mary as, in a special way, "Daughter of Zion." She stands in the long line of faithful women who have been instruments of God's merciful actions down through the ages. The child she is to bear, through the miraculous intervention of the Lord of the Covenant, is "Yeshua"—"Yahweh saves." This woman, so totally of the OT, yet totally of the NT, is the instrument par excellence of all God's chosen instruments for the ultimate expression of the Covenant in the incarnate Son of God.

SOME FACETS OF THE SYMBOL

(a) The Mercy of God

Mary is "the New Eve." Fashioned from clay she plays her role in the history of salvation with utmost fidelity, unlike the first Eve. As the "New Mother" of the "New Adam," Mary reminds us of the essential earthiness of the Incarnation. Freud commented: *"Inter urinas et faeces nascimur"* ("Between urine and faeces we are born"). It is a temptation to reduce life to clearcut, rational and logical units, to forget the earthy origins we all share. Masculinity, typically, would have us leave the earthy (that is the messy and ultimately uncontrollable) side of life behind and live as if we were, in fact, not bodily beings. A woman who has borne a child is less likely to forget that. The natural bonding between mother and child, which can of course be inhibited, even broken, tends towards nurturing and healing dispositions and actions. Such dispositions and actions form a natural basis for the mercy and compassion that permeate the relationship God intends to forge with us, and which in the final analysis make human existence sane and life promoting. It is masculinity dislocated from these dispositions and actions that tends towards merciless and violent movements against self and others.

(b) Sign of the Kingdom

Mary is also Virgin. She gives witness to that Kingdom where "there is no giving and receiving in marriage."[18] Mary as Virgin points to "Home" beyond the "home" she engenders in her motherhood. Her virginity points to the Beyond and the not-yet, in much the same way as her motherhood points to the here and now and the already. The two realities stand in creative tension in Mary, each emphasizing complementary elements of the Pilgrim Church. When the Church avoids that tension and loses a sense of the complementarity, she loses something of her richness and lifegiving potential. As "Mother" the Church provides a "home" of mercy and compassion for wayfarers, as "Virgin" she is a sign of our final "Home." There is always the danger with "virginity"—not so obvious with "motherhood"—of tending towards an idealized world stripped of messiness and its cry for mercy. Life as "virginal," precisely in its "incompleteness," begs for the fruitful relationship for which the human heart cries out, a relationship which no other human can fulfill for us. It is an awful risk and can only be fruitfully lived—never "safely" lived—in the embrace of the Mystery. One only "chooses" virginity in response to the call of the Mystery.

(c) Giving Birth To The Mystery

Mary is "*theotokos*"—"Mother of God." She is the "Ark of the Covenant." Her vocation is pre-eminently that of giving birth to the Mystery in the world. And what other vocation is there for any human being? Fidelity to the Mystery revealed in the Covenants implies that we are all the "Mothers of God." My life is an expression of the Mystery and my responsibility to the world is to *be* that and facilitate the work of the healing and reconciling Mystery in my own life and the world in which I live. As a witness to the Good News—my bounden duty because of baptism—I must live so as to give birth to the Mystery at every point of the journey. Sin is to abort the Mystery.

(d) The Vigor and Joy of Christian Living

There is both freedom and bounce in the life of Mary. "My soul glorifies the Lord, my spirit rejoices in God my savior." Her receptivity is energetic. She responds—rather than reacts—to situations. She is a vigorous and joyful participator in the pilgrimage of faith. Grounded in the wonderful promise of the Covenant, she is able to give herself to "what is," without being lost in or overcome by the ambiguities and tragedies of life. Mary simply believes and believes simply. Yet, she questions, challenges, pursues and searches without denying anything, most especially without denying the essential love and purposefulness of that Mystery which is her lifeblood, and without trying to reduce life to controllable units.

(e) Suffering As Only A Mother Can
At Calvary Mary is "there." Having watched her Son grow and move away from home to pursue the vocation that was his, she encountered the darkness of that journey most horribly on Calvary. She "suffers-with" him. This is "com-passion" at its most real. Nothing can be done except to be "there" in the absurdity of it all and yet hope. There are moments in the lives of us all when there is nothing we can "do," we must simply "be there" in the conviction that our presence is in some way also the presence of the Mystery of everlasting compassion.

(f) Being in and for the Community
At Pentecost Mary is "there," praying with the others. She is "there" as someone energetically receptive to the Mystery working in their midst. Hers is an affirming, supporting spirit. She is not a "nay sayer" or "death dealer." In all its messiness and limitations she is "for" the embryonic Church—she knows what it is to nurture fragile life. She makes no attempt to claim status or position. What is important is the Mystery to be incarnated in this motley, unpretentious human group. She loves the Church—Christ's "body." Just as she nurtured and loved into existence the enfleshed Son of God, so she will do her part to nurture and love into existence the Church.

(g) Living In 'The Belly Of A Paradox'
Thomas Merton referred to himself as "living in the belly of a paradox."[19] Mary is a paradox and she evokes the sense that life is paradox. Paradoxes are apparently contradictory truths which, when held in tension, can reveal realms of reality beyond the boundaries of ordinary language. Mary is mother yet virgin, earthy yet transparent, loving yet not possessive, faithful yet questioning, receptive yet challenging, present yet not intruding, supportive yet not imposing, self-denying yet self-possessed, joyful yet sad, gentle yet determined, energetic yet open. Mary reminds us that life is full of apparent contradictions and absurdities, conflicting truths that only find their resolution beyond the boundaries of human comprehension in the Mystery.

PRACTICAL SUGGESTIONS

(a) Go to a quiet place and read the following text. Meditate on it according to the structure outlined in the Introduction (p.17). Or, alternatively, after praying for some time "with the disciples," see if you can have some kind of "conversation" with Mary the Mother of Jesus. Do not force it. Let it happen. You might find it helpful to use your journal to aid this "conversation."

> Then they returned to Jerusalem from the mount called Olivet, which is near Jerusalem, a sabbath day's journey away; and when they had entered, they went up to the upper room, where they were staying, Peter and John and James and Andrew, Philip and Thomas, Bartholomew and Matthew, James the son of Alphaeus and Simon the Zealot and Judas the son of James. All these with one accord devoted themselves to prayer, together with the women and Mary the mother of Jesus, and with his brothers. . . . When the day of Pentecost had come, they were all together in one place. And suddenly a sound came from heaven like the rush of a mighty wind, and it filled all the house where they were sitting. And there appeared to them tongues as of fire, distributed and resting on each one of them. And they were all filled with the Holy Spirit and began to speak in other tongues, as the Spirit gave them utterance. Acts 1:12–14 and 2:1–4

(b) At odd moments during the week, maybe when you feel particularly harried, frustrated, or just mellow, place yourself with Mary in Nazareth, or Calvary, or Pentecost. Just be there. Listen. Absorb the atmosphere. See if it does not lend perspective to your concrete life situation.

(c) Addressing the symbol that Mary is inevitably brings us face to face with many questions. For instance we could wonder:

> Is it possible to find in God alone a satisfactory resolution of our need to experience and perceive reality as sexually differentiated, as both masculine and feminine? In other words, do we need a feminine symbol to complement the clearly masculine form of Jesus?

> What effect does the decline of Marian devotion and current lack of credible devotional practices centred on Mary have on Christian life formation within the Catholic tradition?

> Is it possible to maintain the symbolism of Mary without credible devotional practices and symbols which focus on her?

> What are the implications, within the Catholic tradition, of having

groups of celibate men and women dedicated explicitly under the patronage of Mary?

In what way has the cult of the Blessed Virgin within the Catholic tradition affected lifestyle, church architecture, liturgical decor and practice?

In what way has the lack of a cult of the Blessed Virgin within the Reformed tradition affected lifestyle, church architecture and worship?

Notes

1 Greeley 1977, p.10.
2 Cf. I. Barbour, *Myths, Models and Paradigms*.
3 Greeley 1977, p.13.
4 Op. cit., p.14.
5 C. Dickson, "Mariology: A Protestant Reconsideration" in *American Ecclesiastical Review*, May 1974, pp.306–7. Cited by A. Greeley, op. cit., p.12. At this point it may be relevant to note the feminine dimensions that are typically present in all the great world religions. For example: in the Chinese tradition there is the "yin"—the shadow, believed to represent the passive, feminine principle of life—and the "yang"—the sun, believed to represent the active, masculine principle of life. The Taoist tradition has also taken over from the Buddhist tradition of India: "Avalokitisvara," the Bodhisatva they call "Kuan Yin" who is the goddess of mercy and compassion. The American Indians see the earth as "mother" and the sun as "father." In the Hindu tradition the deity is spoken of as "he"—"He shining, the sun, the moon and the stars shine after Him" (cited by H. Smith 1965, p.74)—and yet the "black goddess," Kali, (after whom is named the city of Calcutta) is also central.
6 Greeley 1977, p.13.
7 Sexual differentiation is part of the limited human experience of reality which in turn gives certain limits and possibilities to our language. We must, of necessity, speak out of that experience and reflect it in the way we speak. These limits should not be imposed on the object about which we speak. For example, we must speak of God as 'He' or 'She'—each pronoun reflecting our human experience of sexual differentiation but not necessarily implying sexual differentiation in God as such. God is essentially beyond sexual differentiation, yet our language cannot get beyond sexual differentiation without becoming impersonal. Furthermore, this limitation of language calls us to a humble recognition of the limited way in which we struggle to 'name' God for ourselves, both individually and communally. It is quite appropriate, even necessary, to speak within those limits, provided we do not presume that our limited language has in fact grasped the fullness of what we are merely struggling to point towards.
8 See Chapter 2 on "Covenant."
9 Zeph. 3:14–20
10 W. Dalton 1974.
11 Op. cit., p.11.
12 Op. cit., p.12.
13 Rather than delve into all the perspectives of Mary found in the NT, I have chosen to limit the reflections to those given by Luke. The limitations of time and space demand that we set some boundaries. Luke's particular bias gives us plenty to

contemplate and need not lead us to a onesided or distorted view so long as we keep in mind that it is only a partial view—there is much more to Mary than Luke sees. Furthermore we must not forget that Luke writes with an eye to particular details and presents a highly stylized account of the Blessed Virgin in his infancy narratives.

14 Harrington 1969, p.994.
15 Note this same form in the messages to Hagar (Gen. 16:7–15); to the wife of Manoah (Jg. 13:3–20); to Gideon (6:11–24)).
16 Harrington 1969, p.995.
17 Op. cit., p.997.
18 Cf. Mk. 12:25
19 See the foreword in *The Sign Of Jonas*, Hollis and Carter, 1953

12

CONVERSION AS HOMECOMING

"Return, O faithless sons, I will heal your faithlessness." "Behold, we come to thee; for thou art the Lord our God. (23) Truly the hills are a delusion, the orgies on the mountains. Truly in the Lord our God is the salvation of Israel. (24) But from our youth the shameful thing has devoured all for which our fathers labored, their flocks and their herds, their sons and their daughters. (25) Let us lie down in our shame, and let our dishonor cover us; for we have sinned against the Lord our God, we and our fathers, from our youth even to this day; and we have not obeyed the voice of the Lord our God." (Jer. 3:22–5)

Therefore, behold, I will allure her, and bring her into the wilderness, and speak tenderly to her. (15) And there I will give her her vineyards, and make the Valley of Achor a door of hope. And there she shall answer as in the days of her youth, as at the time when she came out of the land of Egypt. (16) And in that day, says the Lord, you will call me, "My husband," and no longer will you call me, "My Ba'al." (17) For I will remove the names of the Ba'als from her mouth, and they shall be mentioned by name no more. (18) And I will make for you a covenant on that day with the beasts of the field, the birds of the air, and the creeping things of the ground; and I will abolish the bow, the sword, and war from the land; and I will make you lie down in safety. (19) And I will betroth you to me for ever; I will betroth you to me in righteousness and in justice, in steadfast love, and in mercy. (20) I will betroth you to me in faithfulness; and you shall know the Lord.
(Hos. 2:14–20)

Now after John was arrested, Jesus came into Galilee, preaching the gospel of God, (15) and saying, "The time is fulfilled, and the kingdom of God is at hand; repent, and believe in the gospel." (Mk. 1:14–16)

ONE CAT, TWO GUNS AND A CHANGING LIFE

The novelist Walker Percy describes a character—Will Barrett—in the midst of a radically changing perception of himself and his world.[1] Will Barrett, whose wife died six months before, has been a most successful business man. He owns a lovely home, a Rolls Royce and a Mercedes Benz. He also owns a Luger and is thinking seriously of suicide one Sunday morning as he sits in his Mercedes:

How, one might ask, could Will Barrett have come to such a pass? Is it not a matter for astonishment that such a man, having succeeded in

139

life and living in a lovely home with a lovely view, surrounded by good cheerful folk, family and friends, merry golfers, should now find himself on a beautiful Sunday morning sunk in fragrant German leather speculating about such things as the odd look of his wrist (his wrist was perfectly normal), the return of North Carolina Jews to the Holy Land (there was no such return), and looking for himself in mirrors like Count Dracula? . . .

. . . As he sat in the Mercedes, Luger in hand, gazing at the cat nodding in the sunlight, there came to him with the force of a revelation the breakthrough he had been waiting for, the sudden vivid inkling of what had gone wrong, not just with himself but, as he saw it, with the whole modern age.[2]

At this point he hears a rifle shot and a bullet "ricocheting with a hideous screech from the concrete floor at his foot to a *thunk* in the brick of the inner wall."[3] Having taken cover he ponders: "Are we afraid quiet afternoons will be interrupted by gunfire? or do we hope they will?"[4] But the gunshot had intruded on his prior meditation:

> As he sat gazing at the cat, he saw all at once what had gone wrong, wrong with people, with him, not with the cat—saw it with the same smiling certitude with which Einstein is said to have hit upon his famous theory in the act of boarding a streetcar in Zurich.
> There was the cat. Sitting there in the sun with its needs satisfied, for whom one place was the same as any other place so long as it was sunny—. . . the cat was exactly one hundred per cent cat, no more, no less. As for Will Barrett, as for people nowadays—they were never one hundred per cent themselves. They occupied a place uneasily and more or less successfully. . . . All too often these days they were two per cent themselves, specters who hardly occupied a place at all. . . . how to restore the ninety eight per cent?[5]

Not all of us are as materially successful in life as Will Barrett. Not all of us own Lugers or seriously consider suicide. There are, however, things happening with Will Barrett that happen, in one form or other, to most of us Western Christians in these times.[6] In the first place, Will Barrett is undergoing a *changing perception of himself and his world*.[7] In the second place, that changing perception is accompanied by a *shifting centre of gravity of his life*.[8] In the third place Will Barrett must make a *decision about the future direction of his life*.[9] It is these three things that we will explore in what follows. In this way we will approach the biblical call to conversion via the common human experience of change. This is not to deny the essential role of grace in the conversion process. It is merely to emphasize the role of the stuff of human existence that gives the truly *human shape* to that experience.

AND THE BLIND SEE

One of the more noticeable characteristics of human life formation is the way our perception of ourselves and our world changes. As forty-year-olds we perceive our parents differently from when we were four-year-olds, especially if we have gone through the parenting process ourselves. Young single men and women tend to have slightly different priorities than young married men and women. The perceptions of a healthy twenty-six year-old are typically different from those of a sixty-six-year-old. That is life.

In a healthy life formation process, that changing of perception is specified in a certain way. It includes a purgation and clarification. We focus with increasing clarity on what matters, we are more and more able to cut through the illusions and distinguish the Real from the real, and the real from the unreal. One of the acid tests of maturity is the ability to see what matters. If the road to hell is paved with good intentions, the road to heaven is paved with useless baggage. Like shrewd antique dealers coming into a flea market, we only see the things of value. Blessed are the clear sighted!

Sometimes it takes great trauma or great effort, or both, to bring about significant, life-altering changes of perception. Often enough, the only way we will come to see what matters is when a relative good is wrenched away from us. Out of the ensuing pain and suffering we might grow a little closer to the truth. Like St Paul we may need to be struck from our horse. Typically, however, it is those moments of ego desperation that hold the seeds of more or less profound change. Our own effortful change too easily brings with it the illusion of ego mastery. And those moments of ego desperation, moments of pain and suffering, may have us discovering the grace inherent there or missing the point altogether. Martin Buber has observed: "The experience of suffering as innocently borne works at times in the history of faith both as a destructive factor and as an element of renewal. *One can endure pain but not the God who sent it: one rejects either him or the image one has made of him.*"[10]

When we have a strong conviction—justifiable or not—that

everything makes sense in our lives and all is more or less under control, we are probably not likely to seek any change. "God is in His heaven, all is right with the world." We are strange that way. Life needs to help us from time to time to change our perceptions of ourselves, God and our world. Consider the following incident from the Gospels:

> And behold, one came up to him, saying, "Teacher, what good deed must I do, to have eternal life?" And he said to him, "Why do you ask me about what is good? One there is who is good. If you would enter life, keep the commandments." He said to him, "Which?" And Jesus said, "You shall not kill, You shall not commit adultery, You shall not steal, You shall not bear false witness, Honor your father and mother, and, You shall love your neighbor as yourself." The young man said to him, "All these I have observed; what do I still lack?" Jesus said to him, "If you would be perfect, go, sell what you possess and give to the poor, and you will have treasure in heaven; and come, follow me." When the young man heard this he went away sorrowful; for he had great possessions.[11]

Jesus' perceptions are unusually deep and rich. They are lifegiving. They determine the direction of his life, as if he is connected to some subterranean stream of Life, able to see the Real beyond the real. The rich young man is perceptive enough to see this much. So he seeks advice from the one who sees clearly what matters. He gets the advice, more than he bargained for. He catches a glimpse and cannot stand it.

That glimpse was the rich young man's chance. Had he been able to hold to that truth shown to him, had he kept looking at that truth long enough for it to find some root in his heart, things might have been different for him. Different also for how many others with whom he might have shared that perception? Perhaps he was not ready for it yet. Perhaps he did come to that point before he died. I hope so.

Once we have allowed ourselves to see, how can we continue as if nothing has happened? Everything looks different in the light of Christ. Contrast the rich young man of the Synoptics with the man born blind in John's Gospel.[12] John's Gospel has many references to light and darkness, seeing and being blind.[13] The detailed description of the incident with the man born blind is one of the more revealing. The physical details are merely "signs" of what is really happening—the real is revealing the Real.

"As he passed by, he saw a man blind from his birth."[14] Jesus is the

Light. He sees first. In him the blind man is about to find his sight. With the transition from not seeing to seeing, this man's whole life will change. He will never be the same again.

"And his disciples asked him, 'Rabbi, who sinned, this man or his parents, that he was born blind?'"[15] The disciples cannot see. They are blinded by a theological interpretation. Like the man born blind, they must have their eyes opened. And this is going on all the time with the disciples. Jesus' presence and teaching means that they will be continually healed of their blindess. This is one of the effects of associating with the Light.

"Jesus spat on the ground and made clay of the spittle and anointed the man's eyes with the clay, saying to him, 'Go, wash in the pool of Silo'am' (which means Sent). So he went and washed and came back seeing."[16] Once again, the real reveals the Real. The ordinary stuff of life—and you cannot get much more ordinary than clay and spit—are the sacraments of the Beyond. How can you see the Lord of Light if you cannot see the dirt between your toes?

"The neighbors and those who had seen him before as a beggar, said, 'Is not this the man who used to sit and beg?'"[17] Light spreads. Other people are drawn into the debate. Some see that the world around them has changed. Some do not believe what they see. Denial begets blindness. Nothing changes for them. Wider horizons emerge and for some it is promise and they are thrilled. For some it is threat and they anxiously run off to the Pharisees. Meanwhile, the miracle is finding deeper roots in the man himself. The turmoil and debate help him to see even more clearly. "He said, 'I am the man.'"[18] Perhaps for the first time in his life, this man begins to see and name himself. The real miracle has begun! He speaks confidently and with disarming honesty in the light of his new perception. He is one of the first human beings to actually see into the heart of Jesus—"He is a prophet."[19]

> "They said to him, 'What did he do to you? How did he open your eyes?' He answered them, 'I have told you already, and you would not listen. Why do you want to hear it again? Do you too want to become his disciples?' And they reviled him, saying, 'You are his disciple, but we are disciples of Moses. We know that God has spoken to Moses, but as for this man, we do not know where he comes from.' The man answered, 'Why, this is a marvel! You do not know where he comes from, and yet he opened my eyes. We know that God does not listen

to sinners, but if any one is a worshipper of God and does his will, God listens to him. Never since the world began has it been heard that any one opened the eyes of a man born blind. If this man were not from God, he could do nothing.' They answered him, 'You were born in utter sin, and would you teach us?' And they cast him out."[20]

If there was a single passage from the Gospels that proved their validity, this could be it. It is wonderfully naive and wise. The insight of the man born blind contrasts starkly with the confusion and utter blindess of the teachers and leaders of the people. This man is changing within himself and changing the world around him. Nothing will ever be the same for him or anyone who comes in contact with him. His logic is compelling, his simple honesty bewildering. He is transparent, one through whom the Light shines. The Pharisees are opaque—not much light shining anywhere there.

"Jesus heard that they had cast him out, and having found him he said, 'Do you believe in the Son of man?' He answered, 'And who is he, sir, that I may believe in him?' Jesus said to him, 'You have seen him, and it is he who speaks to you.' He said, 'Lord, I believe'; and he worshipped him."[21]

The miracle has clearly taken deep root. It will never cease in this man's life. He will go on seeing more and more. What became of this man? Surely he must have gone on seeing more and more and shedding light for others to see. He could not possibly have continued as if nothing had happened. This man is transformed and transforming. Like a sacrament he points beyond himself.

THE SHIFTING CENTER OF GRAVITY

One of the foundational paradoxes of human life formation is put before us in a metaphor by Jesus: "Truly, truly, I say to you, unless a grain of wheat falls into the earth and dies, it remains alone; but if it dies, it bears much fruit. He who loves his life loses it, and he who hates his life in this world will keep it for eternal life."[22] The central truth of transcendence is in direct contrast to the central truth of pride found in the Adam and Eve metaphor.[23] The center of human existence[24] is outside, beyond the person. I only become who I most deeply am by a process of dying to self. Healthy life formation is a constant process of a shifting center of gravity, as it were.

Mary, the Mother of Jesus says: "Behold, I am the handmaid of the Lord; let it be done to me according to your word."[25] John the Baptist says:

"No one can receive anything except what is given him from heaven. . . . I am not the Christ, but I have been sent before him. He who has the bride is the bridegroom; the friend of the bridegroom, who stands and hears him, rejoices greatly at the bridegroom's voice; therefore this joy of mine is now full. He must increase, but I must decrease."[26]

Paul says: "I have been crucified with Christ; it is no longer I who live, but Christ who lives in me; and the life I now live in the flesh I live by faith in the Son of God, who loved me and gave himself for me."[27]

What do I say? What is my experience? Do I know what transformation is, to have the center of gravity shift in my life? Like Victor Hugo's Jean Valjean who is transformed by his encounter with the saintly Monseigneur Bienvenu:

Obscurely he (Valjean) perceived that the priest's forgiveness was the most formidable assault he had ever sustained; that, if he resisted it his heart would be hardened once and for all, and that if he yielded he must renounce the hatred which the acts of men had implanted in him during so many years, and to which he clung. . . . How long did he stay weeping? What did he then do and where did he then go? We do not know. But it is said on that same night the stage-driver from Grenoble, passing through the cathedral square in Digne at three in the morning, saw in the shadows the figure of a man kneeling in the attitude of prayer outside the door of Monseigneur Bienvenu.[28]

The shifting of gravity is an ongoing process. When it has shifted substantially and we find the center of ourselves substantially beyond our egos, certain things become repugnant, even impossible to us. Nikos Kazantzakis gives us a powerful example of this in his autobiographical novel, *Report to Greco*. The Greek narrator in the course of his geographical journey engages in a spiritual journey, a process of discovery and conversion. Towards the end of that journey he tells of an incident in Germany where he attempted something he knew was wrong:

Next to me (in the movie theatre) sat a girl. Her breath smelled of cinnamon. I felt her bosom heave as she respired. From time to time her knee touched mine. I shuddered, but did not draw away. She turned and glanced at me for an instant, and in the half-darkness of the auditorium I thought I saw her smile.

Soon I had enough of watching these shadows, and I got up to
leave. The girl got up also. At the exit she turned again and smiled at
me. We struck up a conversation. The moon shining above us, we
headed toward the park and sat down on a little bench. It was summer;
the night was sweet as honey, the lilacs fragrant. Couples kept passing;
others were embracing, stretched out on the grass. A nightingale
hidden deep in the lilacs began to sing above our heads, and my heart
stood still. It was not a bird; it must have been some cunning goblin.
I had heard this same voice once before, I believe—when climbing
Psiloriti—and I knew what it was saying. Extending my hand, I rested
it on the girl's hair.

"What's your name?" I asked her.

"Frieda," she replied, laughing. "Why ask? My name is 'Woman.' "

At that point something terrible escaped my lips. The words I
spoke were not my own; they must have belonged to one of my
ancestors—not my father, who despised women, but someone else. The
moment I uttered them, I felt overcome by terror. But it was too late.

"Frieda, will you spend the night with me?"

The girl calmly replied, "Not tonight. I can't. Tomorrow."

Feeling relieved, I rose in great haste. We parted. I walked
hurriedly back to my room.

And then something incredible happened, something which
makes me shudder even now when I recall it. Man's soul is truly
indestructible, truly august and noble, but pressed to its bosom it
carries a body which grows daily more putrescent. While on my way
back home, I heard the blood mounting to my head. My soul had
become enraged. Sensing that my body was about to fall into sin, it had
bounded to its feet, full of scorn and anger, and refused to grant
permission. The blood continued to flow upward and mass in my face,
until little by little I became aware that my lips, cheeks, and forehead
were swelling. My eyes soon grew so small that nothing remained but
two slits, and it was only with difficulty that I managed to see anything
at all.

Constantly stumbling, I increased my pace and ran anxiously
homeward in order to look in the mirror and see what state I was in.

When I finally arrived and turned on the light and looked, I
emitted a cry of terror. My entire face was swollen and horribly
disfigured; my eyes were barely visible between two overflowing masses
of florid flesh, and my mouth had become an oblong slot incapable of
opening. Suddenly I remembered the girl Frieda. Being in such a
disgusting state, how could I see her the next day? I wrote out a

telegram: "Can't come tomorrow, will come the day after," and fell onto my bed in despair. What disease can this be? I asked myself. Was it leprosy? As a child in Crete I often saw lepers with their swollen, blood-red, constantly desquamating faces, and now I recalled what horror they had roused in me—so much that one day I had said, "If I were king, I would take all the lepers, hang stones around their necks, and heave them into the sea." Was it possible that the Invisible (*an* Invisible) had remembered my inhuman words and sent me this horrible disease as a punishment?

That night I did not get a moment's sleep. I was anxious for dawn to come, for I said to myself that perhaps the trouble would pass by morning, and I continually investigated my face to see if the swelling had begun to subside. At daybreak I jumped out of bed and ran to the mirror. An appalling mask of flesh was glued to my face; the skin had commenced to burst open and exude a yellowish-white liquid. I was not a man, I was a demon.

I called for the chambermaid in order to give her the telegram. She screamed and hid her face behind her palms the moment she opened the door and saw me. Not daring to come close, she snatched the telegram and left. A day went by, two, three; a week, two weeks. Every day, afraid that the girl might come to my room and see me, I dispatched the same telegram: "Can't come today, will come tomorrow." I felt not the slightest pain, but I could not open my mouth to eat; my only nourishment was milk and lemonade, which I sucked in through a straw. Finally I could stand it no longer. I had read several psychoanalytical works by the famous disciple of Freud, Wilhelm Stekel, and I went to seek him out. My psyche had inflicted this disease on me, though I did not know why. This much I divined: my psyche was to blame.

The learned professor began to hear my confession. I related my life history: how I'd been searching for a path of salvation ever since my adolescence; how I followed Christ for many years, but lately had found His religion too unsophisticated, too optimistic, and had left Him to follow the path of Buddha. . . .

The professor smiled.

"To search in order to find the world's beginning and end is a disease," he said to me. "The normal person lives, struggles, experiences joy and sorrow, gets married, has children, and does not waste his time in asking whence, whither, and why. But you did not finish your story. You are still hiding something from me. Confess everything."

I related how I met Frieda, and said we had arranged a tryst.

The professor burst into shrill, sarcastic laughter. I glanced at him with irritation. I had already begun to hate this man, because he was examining my secrets beneath his indiscreet magnifying glass, and struggling to force open all the barred and padlocked doors inside me.

"Enough! Enough!" he said, beginning to titter again in his sarcastic way. "This mask will remain glued to your face as long as you stay in Vienna. The disease you have is called the ascetics' disease. It is extremely rare in our times, because what body, today, obeys its soul? Have you ever read the saints' legends? Do you remember the ascetic who left the Theban desert and ran toward the nearest city because the demon of fornication had suddenly mounted him, and he felt compelled to sleep with a woman? He ran and ran, but just as he was about to pass through the city gates, he looked down and saw with terror that leprosy was spreading over his body. It was not leprosy, however; it was this disease, the same one you have. With such a revolting face, how could he present himself before a woman? What woman would find it possible to touch him? So he ran back to his hermitage in the desert and gave thanks to God for having delivered him from sin, whereupon God, according to the legend, forgave him and scraped the leprosy off his body. . . Do you understand now? Plunged as it is in the Buddhist Weltanschauung, your soul—or rather what for you goes by the name of soul—believes that sleeping with a woman is a mortal sin. For that reason it refuses to permit its body to commit this sin. Such souls, souls capable of imposing themselves to so great a degree on the flesh, are rare in our age. In my entire scientific career I have encountered only one other such case, that of an extremely upright, extremely pious Viennese lady. She loved her husband very much, but he was away at the front, and she chanced to meet a young man and fall in love with him. One night she was ready to surrender herself, but suddenly her soul rose up in revolt, opposing her. Her face became repulsively swollen, just as yours is now. In desperation she sought me out. I reassured her. 'You'll be cured when your husband comes back from the war,' I told her, and indeed, as soon as her husband returned, in other words as soon as the danger of sin was past, her face regained its original beauty. Your case is the same. You will be cured as soon as you depart from Vienna and leave Frieda behind you."

I did not believe it. Scientific fairy tales, I said to myself, leaving in a state of stubborn vexation. I'll stay in Vienna, I'll stay and get better. . . I remained for another month, but the mask did not melt away.

I continued to send the daily telegram to Frieda: "Can't come today, will come tomorrow." This tomorrow never arrived, however. One morning, having grown weary of the whole business, I got out of bed with the resolute determination to leave. I took my valise, descended the stairs, emerged into the street, and headed for the station. It was early morning and a cool breeze was blowing. Working-class men and women were racing to their jobs in merry flocks, still munching mouthfuls of bread. The sun had not come down into the streets yet. Several windows were being opened; the city was awakening. I walked with weightless steps, in a fine mood; I was awakening just like the city. I felt my face losing its burden as I proceeded. My eyes were being freed, they could open now. The swelling in my lips began to subside, and I started whistling like a child. The cool breeze passed over my face like a compassionate hand, like a caress. When I finally reached the station and took out my pocket mirror to look at myself, what joy, what good fortune! The swelling in my face had entirely disappeared; my former features—nose, mouth, cheeks—had returned. The demon had fled; once more I was a human being.

Ever since that day I have realized that man's soul is a terrible and dangerous coil spring. Without knowing it, we all carry a great explosive force wrapped in our flesh and lard. And what is worse, we do not want to know it, for then villainy, cowardice, and falsehood lose their justification; we can no longer hide behind man's supposed impotence and wretched incompetence; we ourselves must bear the blame if we are villains, cowards, or liars, for although we have an all-powerful force inside, we dare not use it for fear it might destroy us. But we take the easy, comfortable way out, and allow it to vent its strength little by little until it too has degenerated to flesh and lard. How terrible not to know that we possess this force! If we did know, we would be proud of our souls. In all heaven and earth, nothing so closely resembles God as the soul of man.[29]

Perhaps this is what Saul experienced in his bouts of rage and despondency,[30] David in his desolation over the death of Bathsheba's son,[31] Jeremiah when he tried to avoid his call[32]. Perhaps the pagan poet Horace (65–8 BC) had something like that in mind when he wrote: "*Naturam expellas furca, tamen usque recurret.*"[33] I wonder are there any around today who are passionate enough about their commitment to the person and teaching of Jesus Christ to get sick when they act—or attempt to act—contrary to that commitment? To what extent is any sickness a dis-ease of spirit?

DECIDING ABOUT FUTURE DIRECTIONS

Conversion is homecoming. That is, the call of the Gospels "to repent"[34] is a call to hear and heed the truth for which we are made, the truth which we are in Christ. The Light and Truth is in our midst, we should submit and conform our lives to that Light and Truth, for that is why we exist, that is where we find our true selves. Anything contrary to that is not of the light, it is a lie. We are being called home to the truth of who and what we most deeply are. The person and teaching of Jesus is a revelation of what is, not an imposition of something alien. The call to conversion is nothing more nor less than a call to obey the deepest longings of the human heart being met by the grace of God in Christ.

We must co-operate. The choice is ours. In the reference to the little girl in Auschwitz[35] Frankl goes on to say:

> We have stated that that which was ultimately responsible for the state of the prisoner's inner self was not so much the enumerated psychophysical causes as it was the result of a free decision. Psychological observations of the prisoners have shown that only the men who allowed their inner hold on their moral and spiritual selves to subside eventually fell victim to the camp's degenerating influences.[36]

In the depths of our beings we are gifted with the potential to choose to seek truth, or choose to ignore that. Every decision we make, implicitly or explicitly, has something to do with our conversion. Every decision helps or hinders our ability to perceive more clearly, to promote the shifting centre of gravity to the One who is Life. Conversion does not just "happen." Nor does it happen "once for all." Understood as central to the very process of human existence, it is either being promoted or obstructed throughout our lives. In specifically Christian terms, conversion involves an increasing ability to see the world as Christ does, an increasing sense that Christ—not my ego—is the centre of all that I am and am called to be, and increasing conviction that I must choose to co-operate with grace and facilitate this process of never ending change.

PRACTICAL SUGGESTIONS

a) Go apart to some quiet place. Sit still. Pray a "Here I am" prayer ("Here I am Lord, I feel . . . I am concerned about . . . this is on my mind . . . etc. . . . I give this time to you"). After a few moments of stillness following the "Here I am prayer" take pen and paper and write down the significant turning points in your life. Do not rush it. Allow the different events to emerge and name themselves. The *process* is more important than the *accuracy* of the process. When you have finished put your pen down and sit in silence. Pray as you feel led to pray. Or simply sit and be still with what emerges. Conclude with an appropriate prayer.

b) Using the meditation method outlined in the Introduction (p.17), meditate on "The Temptations in the Desert" (Mt. 4:1–11).

c) If someone from outside the Christian tradition were to ask you what difference Christ makes in your life today, what would you say?

Notes

1 Walker Percy 1980.
2 Op. cit., p.12.
3 Op. cit., p.15.
4 Op. cit., p.16.
5 Ibid.
6 "(Will Barrett) lived in the most Christian nation in the world, the USA, in the most Christian part of that nation, the South, in the most Christian state in the South, North Carolina, in the most Christian town in North Carolina." (Op. cit., p.13.)
7 One of the first things we learn about Will Barrett is that "the world and life around him . . . seemed to grow more senseless and farcical with each passing day." (Op. cit., p.3).
8 Will Barrett speaks of "seeing onself as a man among men rather than a self sucking everything into itself." (Op. cit., p.14).
9 The question—"How to restore the ninety eight per cent?"—demands some kind of decisive response from Will Barrett. The rest of the book is, in one way or another, a record of Will Barrett's struggle with that question and the response it begs.
10 Martin Buber 1986, p.143. The emphasis is mine. Victor Frankl describes the response of a young girl in Auschwitz that shows the remarkable human capacity to transcend even the most horrible situations: "'I am grateful that fate has hit me so hard,' she told me. 'In my former life I was spoiled and did not take spiritual accomplishments seriously.' Pointing through the window of the hut, she said, 'This tree here is the only friend I have in my loneliness.' Through that window she could see just one branch of a chestnut tree, and on the branch were two blossoms. 'I often talk to this tree,' she said to me. I was startled and didn't quite know how to take her words. Was she delirious? Did she have occasional hallucinations? Anxiously I asked her if the tree replied. 'Yes.' What did it say to her? She answered, 'It said to me, 'I am here—I am here—I am life, eternal life.'" (1974, p.69).
11 Mt. 19:16–22. See also Mk. 10:17–31; Lk. 18:18–30.
12 Cf. Jn. 9:1–38.
13 Consider, for example, the following references taken from just the first chapter of John's Gospel: "In him was life, and the life was the light of men. The light shines in the darkness, and the darkness has not overcome it." (4,5) "I myself did not know him; but he who sent me to baptize with water said to me, `He on whom you see the Spirit descend and remain, this is he who baptizes with the Holy Spirit.' And I have seen and have borne witness that this is the Son of God." (33, 34) "He said to them,

'Come and see.' They came and saw where he was staying; and they stayed with him that day, for it was about the tenth hour." (39) "Nathan'a-el said to him, 'Can anything good come out of Nazareth?' Philip said to him, 'Come and see.'" (46) "Jesus answered him, 'Because I said to you, I saw you under the fig tree, do you believe? You shall see greater things than these.' (51) And he said to him, 'Truly, truly, I say to you, you will see heaven opened, and the angels of God ascending and descending upon the Son of man.'"(50, 51) The contrasting of light and darkness is a common one in religious literature of the time. Cf."Light" in the Index of *The New Jerome Biblical Commentary*, ed. Raymond Brown, Prentice Hall, 1990.

14 Jn. 9:1.
15 Jn. 9:2.
16 Jn. 9:6f.
17 Jn. 9:8ff.
18 Jn. 9:9.
19 Jn. 9:17.
20 Jn. 9:26–34.
21 Jn. 9:35–8.
22 Jn. 12:24–5.
23 Cf. Gen. 3:1ff.
24 The English word *exist* comes from the Latin words "*ex*" and "*stare*," meaning "to stand outside." Existence understood in this strict etymological sense only applies to human persons. Animals, plants and inanimate things do not *exist* in this sense of transcendence, of finding their identity beyond themselves.
25 Lk. 1:38.
26 Jn. 3:27–30.
27 Gal. 2:20.
28 Hugo 1987, pp.116, 118.
29 Kazantzakis 1989, pp.353–7. This incident is not unlike Ivan's illness towards the end of Dostoievsky's *The Brothers Karamazov*, pp.771–96. The younger brother Alyosha comments on the illness: "The anguish of a proud determination. An earnest conscience!" (p.796).
30 For example: "And on the morrow an evil spirit from God rushed upon Saul, and he raved within his house . . ." 1Sam. 18:10
31 "David therefore besought God for the child; and David fasted, and went in and lay all night upon the ground. (17) And the elders of his house stood beside him, to raise him from the ground; but he would not, nor did he eat food with them." 2Sam. 12:16–17
32 "O Lord, thou hast deceived me, and I was deceived; thou art stronger than I, and thou hast prevailed. I have become a laughingstock all the day; every one mocks me. (8) For whenever I speak, I cry out, I shout, 'Violence and destruction!' For the word of the Lord has become for me a reproach and derision all day long. (9) If I say, 'I will not mention him, or speak any more in his name,' there is in my heart as it were a burning fire shut up in my bones, and I am weary with holding it in, and I cannot." Jer. 20:7–9
33 *Epistles*, I, x, 24. Roughly translated: "If you pitchfork nature out, even so it will return." Dostoievsky puts similar words on the lips of the defense lawyer Fetyukovitch in *The Brothers Karamazov*: "Drive nature out of the door and it will fly in the window" (p.904).
34 Cf. Mt. 11:20; Mk. 1:4, 15 etc.
35 See footnote 10.
36 Frankl 1974, p.69.

13

ABANDONMENT AND PILGRIMAGE

Then God said, "Let us make man in our image, after our likeness; and let them have dominion over the fish of the sea, and over the birds of the air, and over the cattle, and over all the earth, and over every creeping thing that creeps upon the earth." (27) So God created man in his own image, in the image of God he created him; male and female he created them. (Gen. 1:26–7)

My soul longs, yea, faints for the courts of the Lord; my heart and flesh sing for joy to the living God. (Ps. 84:2)

My desire is to depart and be with Christ. (Phil. 1:23)

HUMANS CAN BE WISTFUL AT TIMES

What is it about the following experiences that can arouse in us a more or less strong affective response:

- going home?
- leaving home?
- saying goodbye?
- the sight of stranded travellers at the airport?
- a line of traffic moving along the open highway at night?
- waiting for someone to arrive from a long trip?
- meeting someone from home when you are a long way from home?
- the sound of a train in the distance at night?
- the passing throng with their luggage in a rail terminal?
- being housebound by illness or weather?

Why do young people choose to leave the security and comfort of an affluent situation and backpack around the world? What possesses a middle-aged man to forsake his family and move in with his twenty-two year-old secretary? Why is the traditional hero of the Westerns—typically a celibate who comes from nowhere and moves on—an attractive character to so many? Why do people subject themselves to the torments of running marathons? What is it about the reality of impermanence, novelty and change in life that we can find seductive yet distressing? Why are we never completely satisfied by anything? What could Oscar Wilde mean by saying that there is only one thing worse than not having one's expectations satisfied, that's having them satisfied? Why does the theme of "arduous journeys" appear so frequently in mythology?[1] Why is St Augustine's *Confessions* even more popular now than when he wrote it sixteen hundred years ago? Why do people so frequently quote the first lines of the *Confessions*—"Our hearts are restless . . ."—with approval? Why did the Fathers find Plato's reflection on human life as "living in the land of unlikeness" so meaningful?

Clearly there are no "answers" to these questions. Yet they all, in different ways, open us to a powerful and often disturbing reality about our situation as human beings: *We are a paradox—beings who, at one level of our existence, long to settle down, and, at another level of our existence, long to move on.* We cannot help ourselves. Try as we might to freeze a pleasant moment, we know both that we cannot and (deep down) that we do not want to. We must move on and (deep down) we want to move on beyond this moment, this event. Yes we even want to move beyond our very selves. In the very moment of "arriving" there are always the seeds of the "not yet having arrived." We long to be "home," somewhere, but we never quite get there.

Human life formation is always "in-between." It is *relational*—always "in-between" subject and object (ourselves and ourselves, ourselves and other people, events and things). It is also *movement*—always "in-between" events, the "now" and the "not-yet."[2]

Consider the following: Near the beginning of Walker Percy's novel, *Love in the Ruins*, the central character and storyteller, Dr Tom Moore, reflects:

> The sand trap and the clouds put me in mind of being ten years old and in love and full of longing. The first thing a man remembers is longing and the last thing he is conscious of before death is exactly the same longing. I have never seen a man die who did not die in longing. When I was ten years old I woke one morning to a sensation of longing. Besides the longing I was in love with a girl named Louise, and so the same morning I went out to this same sandtrap where I hoped chance would bring us together. At the breakfast table I took a look at my father with his round head, his iron-colored hair, his chipper red cheeks, and I wondered to myself: at what age does a man get over his longing?[3]

Martin Heidegger has observed:

"University philosophers will never understand what Novalis said: 'Philosophy is, strictly speaking a homesickness." It is not a discipline that can be learned. . . . He who does not know what homesickness is, cannot philosophise if—and because—we do not feel at home anywhere, because we are unceasingly being pushed up against Being, against that because we feel at home nowhere except on the way to the total and essential. We are without a native land and are restlessness itself, living restlessness; it is because of this that it is necessary for us to philosophise. . . . And we are not allowed to let it pass away, to comfort ourselves in an illusion about totality and a satisfactory infinitude. We must not only bear this restlessness in us, but accentuate it, . . . only then are we in a position to be "gripped." And when we thus make ourselves "grippable," by handing ourselves over to reality, our homesickness makes us into human beings.[4]

As an Epilogue to his book, *The Devils of Loudun*, Aldous Huxley notes:

Without an understanding of man's deep-seated urge to self-transcendence, of his very natural reluctance to take the hard, ascending way, and his search for some bogus liberation either below or to one side of his personality, we cannot hope to make sense of our own particular period of history or indeed of history in general, of life as it was lived in the past and as it is lived today. . . . Always and everywhere, human beings have felt the radical inadequacy of their personal existence, the misery of being their insulated selves and not something else, something wider, something in Wordsworthian phrase, "far more deeply interfused."[5]

Josef Pieper writes: "The entire energy of human nature (can be conceived of as) a hunger which demands salvation, a thirst that requires quenching."[6]

Martin Buber writes:

The profane is now regarded only as a preliminary stage of the holy; it is the not-yet-hallowed. But human life is destined to be hallowed in all its natural, that is, created structure. "God dwells where one lets Him in" says a Hasidic saying; the hallowing of man means this letting in. Basically the holy in our world is nothing other than what is open to transcendence, as the profane is nothing other than what is at first closed off from it, and hallowing is the event of opening out. Here a misunderstanding must be avoided. One readily ascribes to Judaism a "religious activism" which does not know the reality of grace and pursues vain self-hallowing or self-salvation. In reality, in Judaism, the relation between man's action and God's grace is guarded as a mystery, even as that between human freedom and God's all-knowing, a mystery which is ultimately identical with that of the relation betwen God and man. Man cannot take himself in hand, so to speak, in order to hallow himself: he is never in his own hand. But there is something that he has retained as a creature, something that is given over just to him and expected just from him; it is called the beginning. A saying explains the opening word of the Hebrew Bible, the word "b'reshit," "In the beginning," in this fashion: the world was created for the sake of the beginning, for the sake of making a beginning, for the sake of human beginning-ever-anew. The fact of creation means an ever renewed situation of choice. Hallowing is an event which commences in the depths of man, there where choosing, deciding, beginning take place. The man who thus begins enters into the hallowing. But he can only do this if he begins just as man and presumes to no superhuman holiness. Therefore the Biblical command, "Holy men shall you be unto me" has received the interpretation thus: "*Humanly* holy shall you be unto me."[7]

THE BIBLE REVEALING US TO OURSELVES

Buber's reflections above lead us into the light of divine revelation. We began this book with the observation that biblical revelation does not add anything to reality, let alone impose something alien to human existence, so much as reveal what is there. If movement, journeying and longing and so on are genuine themes of human existence—part of what is—we can expect the Bible to reflect this. And it most certainly does.

The two pivotal Events that are, as it were the lodestones or gyroscopes of biblical revelation, are the Exodus in the OT and the Passover in the NT. Both are movements or journeys—from, through, towards.

The promise given to Moses[8] focuses initially on God's action: God promises to "deliver" the people, to "bring them up" out of Egypt and into the Promised Land. The people, however, have to respond in willingness to go where they are being called. They are to eat the symbolic Passover meal as if equipped for a journey.[9] They embark on their arduous journey, moving into the uncharted places of the desert—there God alone knows the way. It is the wilderness of God's very Mystery Presence.[10] The journey is not only liberation from slavery, it is also abandonment to divine providence. To think of the liberating journey outside the context of abandonment to the Mystery, is to miss the whole point of the journey. One does not make sense without the other.

From hereon the people must live in the light of the Promise—"God has liberated his people, but he has liberated them for journey, not for rest."[11] Constant movement is their vocation, movement ever more deeply into abandonment to the life of the Mystery and the Promise. There are times on the journey when the focus shifts and the people lose their groundedness in the Mystery and thus their conviction of the Promise.[12] No longer abandoned to the Mystery—they rather feel abandoned by the Mystery—they look to finite material sources, "idols," to give them life and direction and security. They even grow nostalgic about "the good old days" in Egypt.[13] Yet Moses and the leaders who follow him in the subsequent generations always call the people back to their primary vocation to live in the light of the Promise, to never settle for anything less, to always be abandoned in the end to the Mystery Presence no matter what the immediate situation was like, no matter what the cost.

Jesus' whole identity, as portrayed for us in the Gospels, hinges on the journey to Jerusalem and the Passover which he must suffer. Jesus "resolutely took the road to Jerusalem";[14] He has "nowhere to lay his head";[15] His "meat" is to do the will of the One who sent Him.[16] Jesus, foreshadowed by the people of old in their journey out of Egypt into the desert, obedient to the will of the Father, must make his own journey into the desert of Calvary—the wilderness of the Mystery Presence. Unlike the people of old, Jesus is utterly faithful in abandoning Himself to the will of the Father and makes the journey without deviating. He emerges as the Risen Lord, "the first of many brethren."[17]

Jesus instructs his followers to trust in divine providence[18] and his inner circle of friends who are to pass on his teachings are "apostles"—"those who are sent."[19] These are the first of many generations who will follow Jesus, "the Way."[20]

The Exodus of our ancestors of old, and the Passover of Jesus, are archetypal events. They represent human existence as it is in the plan of God: a journey from slavery to freedom, a living in the light of a Promise, a homecoming. Both events reveal to us the meaning of the inherent longing and yearning that agitates and at times torments us. More than that, Jesus, in his very person, *is* the journey and the Promise. It is by abandoning ourselves to the Spirit of the risen Lord—the Spirit who bears united witness with our spirits that we are children of God[21]—that we make the journey that is ours. Abandonment to the Mystery *is* the journey. However, that journeying is a co-journeying, a being caught up in the Mystery.[22]

PRACTICAL INSIGHTS ARISING

Of the multitude of practical isights that might emerge from the foregoing, we can consider the following: (a) Life as "liminal"; (b) boredom and apathy as a defense against longing and desire; (c) a view of life that is not eschatological is not Christian; (d) the Church is a Pilgrim People.

(a) Life as "Liminal"

The anthropologists Victor and Edith Turner use the term "liminality" (from the Latin *"limen"* meaning "threshold") to assist with the understanding of the phenomenon of pilgrimage in human experience.[23]

> Liminality is the state and process of mid-transition in a rite of passage. During the liminal period, the characteristics of the "liminars" (the ritual subjects in this phase) are ambiguous, for they pass through a cultural realm that has few or none of the attributes of the past or coming state. Liminars are betwixt and between. The liminal state has frequently been likened to death; to being in the womb; to invisibility, darkness, bisexuality, and the wilderness.'[24]

Cultures and religious traditions ritualize this liminal experience that is common to human existence as such. Human life is, in a sense, liminal, always on the threshold, always "betwixt and between." We are always in a state of ambiguity, even if we are not conscious of that fact. The ritualization of the phenomenon does not take it away or simply localize it to one part of life. Such ritualization reminds us that it is one of the enduring facts of life for us all. It will of course emerge more powerfully from time to time. We have our phases in which the illusions of having "arrived" somewhere, of being able to take the world for granted, take over for a time. Life would be hellish if this did not happen to give us some respite. The people of old typify the not so secret desire in all of us—to find our home here and now. The Pharisees, so significant for their fidelity to the tradition during the persecution by the Greeks, found a stern opponent in Jesus because they had settled into a packaged religion that forgot the essential Covenantal reality. Alfred Schutz' observation haunts us: "The taken-for-granted world always carries the rider—'until further notice.'"

(b) Boredom and Apathy as a Defense Against Longing and Desire

Karl Menninger has commented that apathy is the other side of anger. When we cannot bear to face a challenge or conflict we look for an evasion, a way out. To adopt an apathetic or bored mode, albeit unconsciously, gives us an out. The journey of life appears too much for us so we sit down and pretend we do not really care anyhow. To press on beyond the familiar—which breeds contempt—takes effort. It costs us something.

To dare to hope—to give free rein to the longing heart in the light of the Promise—implies the possibility of despair. The Bible demands that we so dare. A Promise is given: "What no eye has seen, nor ear heard, nor the heart of man conceived, what God has prepared for those who love him."[25] What we are made for is ultimately beyond anything we can experience here or even imagine. Strangely enough this is—at least sometimes—a disappointment to most of us. We want it now! We would rather not have to wait and "groan in travail."[26] "To live," says St Augustine in his Commentary on John's Gospel, "is to be exercised by desire." We *live* on desire, on accentuating (as Heidegger pointed out) this very desire and its concomitant restlessness. Desire and longing are part of our very being. To "satisfy" that desire with something less than its Infinite End, is to kill true life. Apathy and boredom are modes of death in life.

The Psalmist paints a vivid picture of the human call to live the desire and longing: "My soul is consumed with longing";[27] "My soul longs, yea, faints for the courts of the Lord";[28] "O God thou art my God, I seek thee, my soul thirsts for thee; my flesh faints for thee, as in a dry and weary land where no water is";[29] "As a hart longs for flowing streams, so longs my soul for thee O God. My soul thirsts for God, for the living God."[30]

(c) A View of Life that is not Eschatological is not Christian

C. S. Lewis writes: "If you read history you will find that the Christians who did most for the present world were those who thought most of the next. . . . Aim at Heaven and you will get earth 'thrown in': aim at earth and you will get neither."[31] That human life is constant movement and change is a conclusion available to natural reason. That human life is a purposeful journey "Home" is a revelation available only to faith (of some kind). One of the most difficult lessons that the people of old had to learn was that God's promise to be with them did not imply military victory, political stability or social harmony. It was a promise to be with them on the way.

Jesus endured the same temptations in the desert.[32] Faced with the choice of the two kingdoms, there is no hesitation in Jesus' replies to the tempter. Even Peter endeavored to distract Jesus from the Kingdom.[33] Jesus response is definite: "Get behind me Satan!" Jesus maintained the "messianic secret" presumably for fear that the people would confuse his vocation with a call to merely political or military action.[34] Jesus could have done extraordinary things as a healer (Why did he not set up some kind of ongoing health care system?), as an insurgent (Why did he not overthrow the Roman military rule?), as a political leader (Why did he not attempt to take control of the Jewish political machinery?). Jesus focused on the Ultimate, the Kingdom. His life's focus does not imply that these other facts of life are irrelevant, just that they are not the Ultimate. He lived for the eschaton and charged His disciples to always live in the light of that same Promise. Whatever else is done, it must be done in the context of and relative to that eschatological Promise.[35]

(d) The Church is a Pilgrim People

The Fathers of the Second Vatican Council spoke of the Church as "sojourning on earth as an exile."[36] "Its goal is the kingdom of God."[37] As "the new Israel which, while going forward in this present world, goes in search of a future and abiding city[38] (cf. Heb. 13:14)."

The Church can never regard herself, her work or her institutional aspects as ends in themselves. She is a group of pilgrims, following in the footsteps of the people of old and Jesus himself, guided and vivified by the Spirit of the risen Lord. She lives and moves in the light of the same Promise foreshadowed in the old Covenant, ratified in the Passover of Jesus. Like the people of old and Jesus himself, the Church travels the human journey, with all that that implies. She knows that the mercy of God, incarnate in her Lord, far surpasses her infidelities and mistakes. She knows that no structures or laws she enacts on this journey can ever abrogate or destroy the ultimate structures of the Covenant and its laws of freedom and love.[39]

160

PRACTICAL SUGGESTIONS

Read the following passage from Gustav Janouch's memories of the Austrian novelist Franz Kafka (1883–1924). Having read the passage spend some time reflecting on your spontaneous reaction before you reflect on Kafka's observations:

> I realized this once when, on the way from the Accident Insurance Institution to the Altstadter Ring, Kafka and I came to a halt at the Jacobskirche, immediately opposite the Teinhof.
> "Do you know this church?" Kafka asked me.
> "Yes. But only superficially. I know it belongs to the Franciscan Minorites nearby but that's all."
> "But you must certainly have seen the hand that hangs from a chain in the church."
> "Yes, several times even."
> "Shall we go and look at the hand together?"
> "I'd like to very much."
> We entered the church, whose three naves enclose one of the largest ecclesiastical areas in Prague. On the left, immediately beside the entrance, there hung from a long iron chain fixed to the roof a smoke-blackened bone, covered with shreds of dried flesh and sinew, which by its appearance might have been the pathetic remains of a human forearm. It was said to have been hacked off a thief in the year 1400, or soon after the Thirty Years War, and to have been hung in the church "in eternal memory" of the incident.
> According to the chronicles, and to a perpetually renewed verbal tradition, the story of this cruel deed was as follows: On one of the subsidiary altars in the church, which even today is still adorned by many side chapels, there stood a carved wooden statue of the Virgin, hung with gold and silver chains. Attracted by such wealth, a demobilized mercenary hid himself in a confessional where he waited for the church to close. Then he left his hiding place, approached the altar, stood on a stool which the verger normally used when lighting the altar candles, stretched out his hand and tried to take hold of the statue's adornments. But his hand was paralyzed. The thief, who had never entered a church before, thought that his hand was being firmly held by the statue. He tried to free himself, but in vain. In the morning he was discovered lying senseless across the stool by the verger, who alarmed the monks. Soon a large crowd of people collected in prayer around the altar, where the statue of the Mother of God still held fast to the terrified figure of the

thief; among them were the Burgomeister and some of the most prominent citizens of the old town. The verger and the monks tried to remove the thief's hand from the statue, but could not. The Burgomeister therefore summoned the hangman, who with one stroke of his sword severed the thief's forearm from his body. Then "the statue likewise released the hand of the thief." The forearm fell to the ground. The thief was bound up and a few days later he was sentenced to a long term of imprisonment for attempting to rob the church; when he had served his sentence he entered the Minorite order as a lay brother. The severed hand was attached to an iron chain in the church near the tombstone of the Prague city councillor Scholle von Schollenbach. On the pillar nearby was hung a primitive pictorial rendering of the event. With an explanatory text in Latin, German and Czech.

Kafka looked hard at the withered remains of the arm for a moment, threw a glance at the text describing the miracle, and left the church. I followed him.

"How dreadful," I said. "Of course, the miracle of the Madonna was merely the effect of cramp."

"But what caused it?" said Kafka.

I said: "Probably some sudden sense of fear. The religious feeling that lay concealed under the thief's greed for the Virgin's treasures was suddenly released by his action. It was stronger than the thief realized. So his hand became paralyzed."

"Precisely" said Franz Kafka, and put his hand under my arm. "The longing for the divine, the sense of shame at the violation of holiness which always accompanies it, men's innate demand for justice—these are mighty and invincible forces, which grow stronger as men try to oppose them. They exert a moral control. A criminal must therefore suppress these forces in himself before he can commit an objectively criminal act. For that reason, every crime is preceded by a spiritual mutilation. In the mercenary who wanted to rob the statue this failed to occur. Therefore his hand became paralyzed. It was crippled by his own need of justice. So to him the executioner's sword-stroke was less dreadful than you imagine. On the contrary; the shock and the pain brought him salvation. The executioner's physical act took the place of spiritual mutilation. It liberated the wretched, unemployed mercenary, who could not even rob a wooden doll, from the cramp of conscience. He could continue to live as a human being." We walked on in silence. Halfway along the little street which ran from the Teinhof to the Altstadter Ring, Kafka suddenly halted and asked: "What are you thinking of?"

"I was wondering whether something like the story of the thief in the Jacobskirche was still possible today," I answered eagerly and looked questioningly at Franz Kafka. But he only drew his eyebrows together. After a few steps he said: "I think—hardly. Today the longing for God and the fear of sin are gravely enfeebled. We have sunk into a morass of presumption. This was shown by the war, in which for years men's moral strength, and themselves with it, was anaesthetized by mere dehumanization. I believe that today the violator of a church would no longer be struck by paralysis. And if such a thing happened, men would not hack away the thief's arm; they would amputate his antiquated moral imagination. They would send him to a lunatic asylum. There they would simply analyze out of existence the archaic moral impulses which had revealed themselves in hysterical paralysis."

I grinned. "The robber of churches would be transformed into the victim of a suppressed Oedipus, or mother, complex. After all he wanted to rob the Mother of God."

"Of course," Kafka agreed. "Today there is no sin and no longing for God. Everything is completely mundane and utilitarian. God lies outside our existence. And therefore all of us suffer a universal paralysis of conscience. All transcendental conflicts appear to have vanished, and yet all of them defend themselves like the wooden figure in the Jacobskirche. We are immobilized. We are completely transfixed. More than that! Most of us are simply glued to the shaky stool of vulgar common sense by the filth of fear. That is our entire way of life. I—for instance, sit in my office in the Accident Insurance Institution, look at documents and try to conceal my distaste for the whole Institution behind an expression of solemnity. Then you appear. We talk about everything under the sun, walk through the noisy streets into the quiet of the Jacobskirche, look at the severed hand and discuss the moral paralysis of our times and I go into my parents' shop for something to eat and write a few polite warning letters to some outstanding debtors. But nothing happens. The world is in order. Only we are transfixed like the wooden figure in the church. But without an altar." He touched me lightly on the shoulder—"Goodbye."[40]

Notes

1   Cf. C. D. Rosenberg 1986, xv.
2   In the newly developing formation science, pioneered by Adrian van Kaam, when researchers take an experience of lived reality to study, they must take account of the "movement" in that experience. There is always a "from," "through" and "towards." Interestingly enough, the "from" and the "towards" are the easier elements to grapple with. The "through" is more elusive and mercurial. There one faces the essential

"movement"—or, more properly, the essential "moving" that one's life is. And it resists the control of our thoughts. In the end it defies all description. It reminds us that human and Christian life formation is a mysterious thing.

3 Percy 1979, p.20f.
4 Heidegger cited in A. Naess 1967, p.174.
5 Huxley 1971, 342f.
6 J. Pieper 1958, p. 32; cited by G. Jordan in "The Dynamics of Human Longing and the Cosmic Epiphany," unpublished dissertation, Duquesne University, Pittsburgh, 1986, p.97. See this same dissertation for further excellent development of similar themes.
7 Martin Buber 1958, pp.29–31.
8 Cf. Ex. 3:7–10.
9 Cf. Ex. 12:11.
10 Cf. Dumm 1987, 61ff.
11 Dumm, op. cit., p.59.
12 Cf. Ex. 32:1–5.
13 Cf. Num. 11:4–6.
14 Lk. 9:51.
15 Mt. 8:20.
16 Jn. 4:34.
17 Rom. 8:9.
18 Cf. Lk. 12:22–32.
19 Lk. 6:13 and Rom. 1:1.
20 Jn. 14:6.
21 Cf. Rom. 8:16.
22 "Not that I have already obtained this or am already perfect; but I press on to make it my own, because Christ Jesus has made me his own." Phil. 3:12 Cf. Also Rom. 16:25; Eph. 1:3–10; Col. 1:26. One of the disconcerting paradoxes of the call to abandonment is that the more we focus on it and attempt to "achieve" it, the less likely it is to be part of our lives. Insidiously it may become an ego project wherein we become the controllers of not being in control, the masters of not being masters . . . It is like being very attached to being detached. Abandonment is a grace. Humanly speaking we will tend to move towards that which we perceive as the most attractive alternative. It is crucial, therefore, that we do everything in our power to dispose ourselves to being captured by the Mystery of Christ as St Paul was. That way we are *drawn* rather than *driven*.
23 Cf. Victor and Edith Turner 1978, p.249.
24 Ibid.
25 1Cor. 2:9.
26 Cf. Rom. 8:22.
27 Ps. 119:20.
28 Ps. 84:2
29 Ps. 63:1.
30 Ps. 42:1f.
31 C. S. Lewis 1977, p.118.
32 Cf. Mt. 4:1ff.
33 Cf. Mt. 16:21–3.
34 For example, Mk. 8:30 and 9:9.
35 Cf. P. Kreeft 1980.
36 "Lumen Gentium," n.14. Cf. also n.6.
37 Op. cit., n.9.
38 Ibid.
39 Cf. C. Charlier 1961, pp.294–8.
40 Janouch 1985, pp.49–52.

APPENDIX A

"LISTENING TO THE PARABLES OF JESUS"[1]

To preach today on the Parables of Jesus looks like a lost cause. Have we not already heard these stories at Sunday School? Are they not childish stories, unworthy of our claims to scientific knowledge, in particular in a University Chapel? Are not the situations which they evoke typical of a rural existence which our urban civilization has made nearly non-understandable? And the symbols, which in the old days awakened the imagination of simple-minded people, have not these symbols become dead metaphors, as dead as the leg of the chair? More than that, is not the wearing out of these images, borrowed from the agricultural life, the most convincing proof of the general erosion of Christian symbols in our modern culture?

To preach today on the Parables of Jesus—or rather to preach the Parables—is indeed a wager, the wager that in spite of all contrary arguments, it is still possible to listen to the Parables of Jesus in such a way that we are once more astonished, struck, renewed, and put in motion. It is this wager which led me to try to preach the Parables and not only to study them in a *scholarly* way, as a text among other texts.

The first thing that may strike us is that the Parables are radically profane stories. There are no gods, no demons, no angels, no miracles, no time before time, as in the creation stories, not even founding events as in the Exodus account. Nothing like that, but precisely people like us: Palestinian landlords traveling and renting their fields, stewards and workers, sowers and fishers, fathers and sons; in a word, ordinary people doing ordinary things: selling and buying, letting down a net into the sea, and so on. Here resides the initial paradox: on the one hand, these stories are—as a critic said—narratives of normalcy, but on the other hand, it is the Kingdom of God that is said to be like this. The paradox is that the *extraordinary* is *like* the *ordinary*.

Some other sayings of Jesus speak of the Kingdom of Heaven: among them, the eschatological sayings, and they seem to point toward something Wholly-Other, to something beyond, as different from our history as heaven is from earth. Therefore, the first thing which may amaze us is that at the very moment we were expecting the language of the myth, the language of the sacred, the language of mysteries, we receive the language of our history, the language of the profane, the language of open drama.

And it is this contrast between the kind of thing *about* which it is spoken—the Kingdom of Heaven—and the kind of thing to which it is compared which may put in motion our search. It is not the religious person in us, it is not the sacred person in us, but precisely the profane person, the secular person who is summoned.

The second step, beyond this first shock, will be to ask what makes sense in the Parables. If it is true—as contemporary exegesis shows—that the Kingdom of God is not compared to the man who . . . to the woman who . . . to the yeast which . . . but to *what happens* in the story, we have to look more closely at the short story itself, to identify what may be paradigmatic in it. It is here that we run the risk of sticking too closely to the sociological aspects which I evoked at the beginning when I said that the situations described in the Parables are those of agricultural activity and of rural life. What makes sense is not the situations as such, but, as a recent critique has shown, it is the *plot*, it is the structure of the drama, its composition, its culmination, its denouement.

If we follow this suggestion, we are immediately led to look at the critical moments, at the decisive turning points in the short dramas. And what do we find? Let us read once more the shortest, the most condensed of all the Parables, Matthew 13, verse 44. Three critical moments emerge: *finding* the treasure, *selling* everything else, *buying* the field. The same threefold division may be found in the two following Parables: Matthew 13:45–6, 47–9.

If we attempt, now, to let these three critical moments expand, so to say, in our imagination, in our feeling, in our thought, they begin to *mean much more* than the apparent practical, professional, economical, commercial transactions told by the story. *Finding* something . . . This simple expression encompasses all the kinds of *encounters* which make of our life the contrary of an acquisition by skill or by violence, by work or by cunning. Encounter of people, encounter of death, encounter of tragic situations, encounter of joyful events. Finding the other, finding ourselves, finding the world, recognizing those whom we had not even noticed, and those whom we don't know too well and whom we don't know at all. Unifying all these kinds of finding, does not the Parable point toward a certain fundamental relation to time? Toward a fundamental way of being in time? I mean, this mode which deserves to be called the Event par excellence. Something happens. Let us be prepared for the newness of what is new. Then we shall "find."

But the art of the Parable is to link dialectically *finding* to two other critical turning points. The man who found the treasure went and sold everything he had and *bought* it. Two new critical points, which we could call after a modern commentator, himself taught by Heidegger: Reversal and Decision. Decision does not even come second. Before Decision, Reversal. And all those who have read some religious texts other than biblical, and even some texts other than religious, know how much has been invested in this word "conversion," which means much more than making a new choice, but which implies a shift in the direction of the look, a reversal in the vision, in the imagination, in the heart, before all kinds of good intentions and all kinds of good decisions and good actions. Doing appears as the conclusive act, engendered by the Event and by the Reversal. First, encountering the Event, then changing one's heart, then doing accordingly. This succession is full of sense; the Kingdom of God is compared to the chain of these three acts: letting the Event blossom, looking in another direction, and doing with all one's strength in accordance with the new vision.

Of course, all the Parables are not built in a mechanical way along the same pattern. If this were the case, they would lose for that very reason the power of surprise. But each of them develops and, so to say, dramatizes one of the other of these three critical terms.

Look at the so-called Parables of Growth: Matthew 13:31–3. This unexpected growth of the mustard seed, this growth beyond all proportion, draws our attention in the same direction as *finding*. The natural growth of the seed and the unnatural size of the growth speak of something which happens to us, invades us, overwhelms us, beyond our control and our grasp, beyond our willing and our planning. Once more the Event comes as a gift.

Some other Parables . . . will lay the stress on the Reversal. Thus the Prodigal Son changes his mind, "reverts" his glance, his regard, whereas it is the father who waits, who expects, who welcomes, and the Event of the encounter proceeds from the conjunction of this Reversal and this Waiting.

In some other Parables, the emphasis will fall on the decision, on the doing, even on the good deed, as in the Parable of the Good Samaritan. But, reduced to the last critical turn, the Parable seems to be nothing more than a moral fable, a mere call to "do the same." Thus reduced to a moral teaching, the Parable ceases to be a Parable of the Kingdom, to become an allegory of charitable action. We have to replace it within the Parables of Event, Reversal, and Decision, if the moral fable is to speak once more as a Parable.

Having made, in that way, this second step and recognized the dramatic structure, the articulation of the plot which makes sense, we are ready for a new discovery, for a new surprise. If we ask: "And finally, what is the Kingdom of Heaven," we must be prepared to receive the following answer. The Gospel says nothing about the Kingdom of Heaven, except that it is *like* . . . It does not say what it *is*, but what it *looks like*. This is hard to hear. Because all our scientific training tends to use images only as provisory devices and to replace *images* by *concepts*. We are invited here to proceed the other way. And to think according to a mode of thought which is not metaphorical for the sake of rhetoric, but for the sake of what it has to say. Only *analogy* approximates what is wholly practical. The Gospel is not alone in speaking in that way. We have elsewhere heard Hosea speaking of Yahweh as the Husband, of Israel as the Wife, of the Idols as the Lovers. No translation in abstract language is offered, only the violence of a language which, from the beginning to the end, *thinks through* the Metaphor and never *beyond*. The power of this language is that it abides to the end *within* the tension created by the images.

What are the implications of this disquieting discovery that Parables allow no translation in conceptual language? At first sight, this state of affairs exposes the weakness of this mode of discourse. But at a second glance, it reveals the unique strength of it. How is it possible? Let us consider that with the Parables we have not to do with a unique story dramatically expanded in a long discourse, but with a full range of short Parables gathered together in the unifying form of the Gospel. This fact means something. It means that the Parables make a whole, that we have to grasp them as a whole and to understand each one in the light of the other. The Parables make sense together. They constitute a network of intersignification, if I dare say so. If we assume this hypothesis, then our disappointment—the disappointment which a scientific mind perceives when it fails to draw a coherent idea, an equivocal concept from this bundle of metaphors—our disappointment may become amazement. Because there is now more in the Parables taken together than in any conceptual system about God and his action among us. There is more to *think through* the richness of the images than in the coherence of a simple concept. What confirms this feeling is the fact that we can draw from the Parables nearly all the kinds of theologies which have divided Christianity through the centuries. If you isolate the Parable of the Lost Coin, if you interrupt the dynamism of the story and extract from it a frozen concept, then you get the kind of doctrine of predestination which pure Calvinism advocated. But if you pick the Parable of the Prodigal Son and extract from it the frozen concept of personal conversion, then you get a theology based on the absolutely free will of man, as in the doctrine that the Jesuits opposed to the Calvinists, or the Protestant Liberals to the Orthodox Protestants.

Therefore, it is not enough to say that the Parables say nothing directly concerning the Kingdom of God. *We must say in more positive terms, that taken all together, they say more than any rational theology.* At the very moment that they call for theological clarification, they start shattering the theological simplifications which we attempt to put in their place. This challenge to rational theology is nowhere more obvious than in the Parable of the Good Seed spoiled by the darnel sowed among the wheat. The farmer's servants went to their master and said, "Sir, was it not good seed that you sowed in your field? Then where has the darnel come from?" Such is the question of the philosopher when he discusses theoretically the so-called problem of evil. But the only answer which we get is itself metaphorical: "This is an enemy's doing." And you may come through several kinds of theologies in agreement with that enigmatic answer. Because there is more to think about in the answer said in a parabolic way than any kind of theory.

Let me propose one more step, a step which I hope will increase our surprise, our amazement. Many people will be tempted to say, "Well, we have no difficulty dropping all systems, including rational or rationalizing theologies." Then, if all theories are wrong, let us look at the Parables as mere practical teaching, as moral or maybe political teaching. If Parables are not pieces of dogmatic theology, let us look at them as pieces of practical theology. This proposal sounds better at first sight than the first one. Is it not said that to listen to the word is to put it into practice? This obviously is true. But what does that mean, to put in practice the Parables?

I fear that a too-zealous attempt to draw immediate application from the Parables for private ethics or for political morality must necessarily miss the target. We immediately surmise that such an indiscreet zeal quickly transposes the Parables into trivial advice, into moral platitudes. And we kill them more surely by trivial moralizing than by transcendent theologizing.

The Parables obviously teach, but they don't teach in an ordinary way. There is, indeed, something in the Parables which we have as yet overlooked and which they have in common with the Proverbs used by Jesus according to the Synoptics. This trait is easy to identify in the Proverbs. It is the use of paradox and hyperbole, in such aphorism and antithetical formulae as: "Whoever seeks to gain his life will lose it, but whoever loses his life will preserve it." As one commentator says, the paradox is so acute in this overturning of fates that it jolts the imagination from its vision of a continuous sequence between one situation and another. Our project of making a totality continuous with our own existence is defeated. For who can plan his future according to the project of losing "in order to win"? Nevertheless, these are not ironical nor skeptical words of wisdom. In spite of everything, life is granted by the very means of this paradoxical path. The same has to be said of hyperbolic orders like: "Love your enemies, do good to those who hate you." Like paradox, hyperbole is intended to jolt the hearer from the project of making his life something continuous. But whereas humor or detachment would remove us from reality entirely, hyperbole leads back to the heart of existence. The challenge to the conventional wisdom is at the same time a way of life. We are first disoriented before being reoriented.

Does not the same happen with the Parables? Is their way of teaching different from that of reorientation by disorientation? We have not been aware enough of the paradoxes and the hyperbole implied in those short stories. In most of them there is an element of extravagance which alerts us and summons our attention.

Consider the extravagance of the landlord in the Parable of the Wicked Husbandman, who after having sent his servants, sent his son. What Palestinian property owner living abroad would be foolish enough to act like this landlord? Or what can we say about the host in the Parable of the Great Feast who looks for substitute guests in the streets? Would we not say that he was unusual? And in the Parable of the Prodigal Son, does not the father overstep all bounds in greeting his son? What employer would pay the employees of the eleventh hour the same wages as those hired first?

The Parables of Growth are no less implausible. Here it is the hyperbole of the proverb that is at work. What small seed would yield a huge tree where birds can nest? The contrast is hardly less in the Parable of the Leaven. As to the Parable of the Sower, it is constructed on the same contrast. If it points to eschatological plenitude, it is because the yield of grain in the story surpasses by far all reality.

The most paradoxical and most outlandish Parables, as far as their realism is concerned, are those which Joachim Jeremias has grouped under the titles, "The Imminence of Catastrophe," and "It may be Too Late." The schema of *occasion*, which only presents itself *one time* and after which it is *too late*, includes a dramatization of what in ordinary experience we call seizing the occasion, but this dramatization is both paradoxical and hyperbolic: paradoxical because it runs counter to actual experience where there will always be another chance, and hyperbolic because it exaggerates the experience of the unique character of the momentous decisions of existence.

At what village wedding has anyone slammed the door on the frivolous maidens who do not consider the future (and who are, after all, as carefree as the lilies of the field)? It is said that, "these are Parables of Crisis." Of course, but the hour of testing and the "selective sorting" is signified by a crisis in the story which intensifies the surprise, the scandal, and sometimes provokes disapproval as when the denouement is "unavoidably tragic."

Let me draw the conclusion which seems to emerge from this surprising strategy of discourse used by Jesus when he told the Parables to the disciples and to the mob. To listen to the Parables of Jesus, it seems to me, is to let one's imagination be opened to the new possibilities disclosed by the extravagance of these short dramas. If we look at the Parables as at a word addressed first to our imagination rather than to our will, we shall not be tempted to reduce them to mere didactic devices, to moralizing allegories. We will let their poetic power display itself within us.

But was not this poetic discussion already at work, when we read the Parable of the Pearl and the Parable of Event, Reversal, and Decision?

Decision, we said, moral decision comes third. Reversal precedes. But the Event opens the path. The poetic power of the Parable is the power of the Event. Poetic means more than poetry as a literary genre. Poetic means creative. And it is in the heart of our imagination that we let the Event happen, before we may convert our heart and tighten our will.

Listen, therefore, to the Parables of Jesus (Matthew 13:31–2 and 45–6)

And another parable he put before them, saying, "The Kingdom of heaven is like a grain of mustard seed which a man took and sowed in his field; it is the smallest of all seeds, but when it has grown it is the greatest of shrubs and becomes a tree, so that the birds of the air come and make nests in its branches."

"Again, the kingdom of heaven is like a merchant in search of fine pearls, who, on finding one pearl of great value, went and sold all that he had and bought it."

Notes

1   Paul Ricoeur, "Listening to the Parables of Jesus," in C. E. Reagan and D. Stewart, eds., *The Philosophy of Paul Ricoeur: An Anthology of His Work*, Beacon Press, 1978, pp.239–45.

APPENDIX B
GUIDELINES FOR HOMILY PREPARATION

THE OPENING DIALOGUE

Read and re-read the texts meditatively, allowing a word, phrase, image, symbol or event to catch your attention. Listen for any reaction, no matter how slight, within yourself.

It might be helpful to pause from time to time, sit back and repeat a word or phrase, ask a question of yourself or the text, listen quietly and gently to the beginnings of some movement within yourself. Then continue reading meditatively.

Be careful to concentrate on *your* relationship with the text. This is a moment where *you* are being interpreted even as you attempt to interpret the text. Be alert to what the text is doing to you. Listen!

Put aside, at this point, any temptation to think about what you would say to others. *Let the text work on you before you start working on it!*

THE EMERGING THEME

When you find some stirring or movement with regard to a particular word, phrase, image, symbol or event, chew on that for awhile. Chances are, that contains a *theme*.

Work with that theme, ask questions that facilitate its emergence as real for you. Go back to the text, keeping an ear to the movement within you, and test the theme. Does it really emerge from the text? What would be the best way to state this theme? Does it carry through each of the texts? In what way?

The theme has a life of its own—let it live!

BEING CAUGHT BY THE THEME

Being "caught" by a particular theme is the essence of the homily preparation. If you are not "caught" you are not likely to be able to communicate a clear and powerful message. The proclaimer of the Word must be an intimate participant in the revealing and healing Word before he or she can enable others to participate in that same revealing and healing conversation between God and the human family.

This "being caught" is a work of grace which we can only facilitate. We do not prepare a homily by mastering a message and fashioning it to fit our audience. The proclaimer is a sacrament of the Word, an instrument of the Spirit. Proclaimers of the Word must submit to the Word and make themselves available to be used by the Word.

Thoughtful reference to commentaries can be a useful part of the facilitation process.

Go back to the texts and re-read them in the light of the theme that has emerged. Is the theme really there? Can I refer to the texts to support my proclamation of this message?

Refine your actual expression of the theme as much as you can. Try to say it in a very simple and straightforward sentence.

The homily then is like an unpacking of that simple sentence. The unpacking can begin with a simple and concise reference to the texts, elaborating and explaining the theme as it is presented there.

A SUPPORTING EXAMPLE

The unpacking of the simple sentence that presents the theme can be greatly assisted by a concrete example. Such examples should promote the theme and not themselves. Sometimes we might be tempted to tell a story, for example, not because it is relevant but simply because it is a good story, or seems so to us. If that happens, the homily serves the story rather than vice versa.

Examples can come from personal experience, stories you have heard or made up, news items, films, novels, things you have been told about. In short, anything that concretizes the theme. There is nothing quite like a good story to do that.

COMING TO A CONCLUSION

There is something particularly painful about watching preachers who cannot conclude. Like nervous pilots approaching the runway, they keep aborting touchdown until they finally run out of fuel and crash.

The preparation of a simple conclusion is an important part of the proclamation. It may be helpful to offer a particular thought for the listener to meditate on, a practical exercise or you may decide that it is appropriate to conclude with the example. (In fact, wouldn't it be interesting to try giving a homily that was simply a story? Tell the story and sit down!) Be inventive, be imaginative. Above all, be definite!

APPENDIX C
BIBLE STUDY GROUPS

[A] THE PURPOSE OF A BIBLE STUDY GROUP

The purpose of such a group is to provide a forum within which adults can learn from:
- the Spirit working in "two or three gathered in (His) name";
- sharing stimulating conversation about important life issues;
- sharing their own lived experiences and considered reflections;
- sharing with others the struggle to integrate life and learning;
- listening to the experiences and reflections of others;

[B] SOME GROUP RULES

The success of the groups presupposes that all members:
- are sensitive to the workings of the Spirit in the group;
- take responsibility for the group's success;
- care for the others in the group;
- endeavor to be there each week and on time;
- prepare material conscientiously;
- are willing to listen and speak;
- maintain the confidentiality of material discussed.

[C] HINTS FOR PARTICIPATING FRUITFULLY IN THE GROUP

Consider the group as having a certain "energy" which must be kept moving. The more the group members share that "energy" or pass it around, the better will the group be. Grace builds on nature—the "Energy" of God with our "energy".

That flow of energy can be inhibited or locked up, for example, by talking excessively, not talking at all, failing to listen sensitively, making cynical or cutting comments, restless body movement, forming sub-groups or alliances, depending too much on the facilitator for promptings, arbitration or answers.

Finding "the answers" or even presuming to search for "the answers" can stifle the group's energy. Questions often enough do have answers and there are teachings of our faith that can be objectively stated. And sometimes a simple answer can help the energy to flow in the group. However, the group will probably be better served if the members are looking for *the questions* they should be asking at this time, rather than the answers. Listen to the others, as they listen to you. Help each other to search for those questions.

The flow of energy can be released and moved, for example by thoughtful and honest comment, sensitive listening, paying attention to the one speaking, encouraging remarks, good humor, gently challenging evasions, allowing people to disagree with you or to share a contrary opinion, claiming the energy respectfully then letting it go.

Focus on the learning possibilities in the group. Even a "bad" group experience is an opportunity to learn.

If the group's energy or your own seems to be chronically inhibited or locked up, address this issue—reflect on what is happening, discuss it with another member of the group or the facilitator or simply raise your concern publicly in the group. Do something about it!

When you see that another member of the group has been distressed, is angry or otherwise has "unfinished business" when the discussion concludes, don't leave that person alone. See that they have some opportunity to express their feelings to someone. However, respect their privacy should they choose not to pursue the matter with you.

[D] LEADERSHIP AND THE VIABILITY OF THE GROUP

Leadership in Bible study groups will typically be unobtrusive. It will focus on facilitating a process whereby the group members are encouraged and, where necessary helped to participate as fully as possible in the formative interaction of the group.

The adults who form the group ought to take responsibility for the group. What the group does and how the group does it lies in the hands of *the group*. That is one of the key dynamics making the groups truly formative.

For this very reason, some groups will thrive and others will disintegrate. Some gatherings of people of certain temperament and predispositions will almost inevitably fail. So be it. There is no value in preserving a group for the sake of preserving a group. There is value in preserving a group—or disbanding it for that matter—*for the sake of Christian life formation.*

BIBLIOGRAPHY

Abbott, W., ed.   *The Documents of Vatican II*, Geoffrey Chapman, 1967.
Allen, W.   *Without Feathers*, Random House, 1975.
Anderson, B.   *Understanding the Old Testament*, Prentice Hall, 1975.
—   *The Unfolding Drama of the Bible*, Fortress Press, 1990.
—   "Sin and the Powers of Chaos" in *Sin, Salvation and the Spirit*, D. Durkin, ed., Liturgical Press, 1979.
Assagioli, R.   *Act of Will*, Penguin Books, 1976.
—   *Psychosynthesis: A Collection of Basic Writings*, Penguin Books, 1977.
Augustine, St   *The Confessions of St Augustine*, J. K. Ryan, trans., Anchor Books, 1969.

Barclay, W.   *New Testament Words*, SCM Press, 1980.
Barrett, W.   *Irrational Man: A Study in Existential Philosophy*, Doubleday Anchor Book, (1958) 1962.
Becker, E.   *The Denial of Death*, Free Press, 1973.
Bellow, S.   *Dangling Man*, Penguin Books, 1988.
Benedict, St   *The Rule of St Benedict*, A. C. Meisel and M. L. del Mastro, trans., Image Books, 1975.
Berger, P. and   *The Social Construction of Reality*, Doubleday, 1966.
   T. Luckmann,
Bernard, St   *The Twelve Steps of Humility and Pride & on Loving God*, H. C. Backhouse, ed., Hodder and Stoughton, 1985.
Blakney, R., trans.   *Meister Eckhart*, Harper Torchbooks, 1941.
Boadt, L.   *Reading the Old Testament*, Paulist Press, 1984.
Böll, H.   *The Stories of Heinrich Böll*, L. Vennewitz, trans., Abacus, 1988.
Boorstin, D.   *The Image: A Guide to Pseudo-Events in America*, Atheneum, 1962.
Bopp, L.   "The Salvific Power of the Word According to the Church Fathers" in *Towards a Theology of the Word: Readings in Theology*, Editor unknown, P. J. Kennedy & Sons, 1964.
Boulding, M.   *Gateway to Hope: An Exploration of Failure*, Fount Paperbacks, 1985.
Bouyer, L.   *A History of Spirituality, Volume I: The Spirituality of the New Testament and The Fathers*, Seabury Press, n.d.
—   *Eucharist: Theology and Spirituality of the Eucharistic Prayer*, University of Notre Dame Press, 1968.
Brown, C.   *The New International Dictionary of New Testament Theology*, Paternolster Press, 1978.

Brown, P.   *Augustine of Hippo: A Biography*, University of
                     California Press, 1969.
Buber, M.   *The Tales of the Hasidim: Later Masters*, Schocken
                     Books, 1948.
—   *Hasidism and Modern Man*, Harper & Row, 1971.
—   *I and Thou*, trans. R. Gregor Smith, Clark, 1952.
—   *The Way of Man According to the Teachings of Hasidism*,
                     The Citadel Press, 1972.
—   *Two Types Of Faith*, N. P. Goldhawk, trans., Colliers,
                     1986.
Bucke, E. S.   *The Interpreter's Dictionary of the Bible*, Abingdon, 1962.
Buechner, F.   *Telling the Truth: The Gospel as Tragedy, Comedy and
                     Fairytale*, Harper, 1977.
Buhlmann, W.   *The Chosen Peoples*, St. Paul Publications, 1982.

Charlier, C.   *The Christian Approach to the Bible*, Sands, 1961.
Clancy, T.   "Feeling Bad About Feeling Good," *Studies in the
                     Spirituality of Jesuits*, XI, 1, January, 1979.
Colledge, E., ed.,   *The Medieval Mystics of England*, Charles Scribner's
                     Sons, 1961.
Cummings, C.   *Monastic Practices*, Dimension Books, 1984.

Dalton, W.   *Mary in the New Testament*, Spectrum, 1974.
Danielou, J.   *Prayer as a Political Problem*, Burns and Oates, 1967.
—   *From Glory to Glory*, Charles Scribner's Sons, 1961.
Dicharry, W.   *To Live the Word Inspired and Incarnate: An Integral
                     Biblical Spirituality*, Alba House, 1985.
Dillard, A.   *Pilgrim at Tinker Creek*, Harper & Row, 1974.
Dostoievsky, F.   *The Brothers Karamazov*, C. Garnett, trans., Modern
                     Library, 1950.
—   *Crime and Punishment*, Random House, Modern Library
                     Edition, 1982.
Dumm, D.   *Flowers in the Desert*, Paulist Press, 1987.

Eco, U.   *The Name of the Rose*, W. Weaver, trans., Harcourt
                     Brace Jovanovich, 1983.
Eliot, T. S.   *The Four Quartets*, Harvest/HBJ, 1971.
Ellis, A. and   *A New Guide to Rational Living*, Wilshire, 1975.
  R. Harper
Ellis, P. F.   *The Men and Message of the Old Testament*, Liturgical
                     Press, 1963.

Farber, L.   *Lying, Despair, Jealousy, Envy, Sex, Suicide, Drugs and
                     the Good Life*, Harper Colophon, 1976.
Fénelon, F.   *Fénelon's Spiritual Letters*, Christian Books, 1982.

Flanagan, M.   "Follow that Vision!" a review of Mary Breasted, Why
                      Should You Doubt Me Now? (Farrar, Straus & Giroux,
                      1993) in *The New York Times Book Review*, November
                      28, 1993.

Fleming, D. L.   *The Spiritual Exercises of St Ignatius: A Literal Translation
                      and a Contemporary Reading*, Institute of Jesuit
                      Resources, 1978.

Frankl, V.   *Man's Search for Meaning*, Hodder and Stoughton, 1974.

Fromm, E.   *To Have or to be*, Jonathan Cape, 1976.

Gardner, J.   *The Sunlight Dialogues*, Vintage Books, 1987.

Gendlin, E.   *Focusing*, Bantam, 1986.

Goldman, A. L.   *The Search for God at Harvard*, Random House, 1991.

Grasso, D.   *Proclaiming God's Message*, University of Notre Dame
                      Press, 1965.

Greeley, A.   *Ecstasy: A Way of Knowing*, Prentice Hall, 1974.

—   *The Mary Myth: The Feminity of God*, Seabury Press, 1977.

Greene, G.   *The Power and the Glory*, Penguin, 1982.

Gregory of Nyssa, St *The Life of Moses*, A. J. Malherbe and E. Ferguson,
                      trans., Paulist Press, 1978.

Guigo II,   *The Ladder of Monks and Twelve Meditations*, Image
                      Books, 1978.

Hall, D. J.   "Rethinking Christ," *Interpretation: A Journal of Bible
                      and Theology*, XXXIII (1979), 254–67.

Harrington, W.   "St Luke" in *A New Catholic Commentary on Sacred
                      Scripture*, Thomas Nelson, 1969, 986–1021.

Hertzberg, A.   *Jewish Polemics*, Columbia University Press, 1992.

Heschel, A.   *Man is not Alone*, Farrar, Straus & Giroux, 1951.

Heschel, A.   *The Prophets, Volume II*, Harper Colophon Books, 1975.

Heschel, A.   *God in Search of Man: A Philosophy of Judaism*, Farrar,
                      Straus and Giroux, 1978.

Hughes, G.   *The God of Surprises*, Darton Longman and Todd, 1985.

Hugo, V.   *Les Misérables*, N. Denny, trans., Penguin Classics, 1987.

Huxley, A.   *The Devils of Loudun*, Harper and Row, 1971.

Janouch, G.   *Conversations with Kafka*, G. Rees, trans., Quartet, 1985.

Jensen, J.   *God's Word to Israel*, Michael Glazier, 1982.

Johnson, W.,Trans.   *The Cloud of Unknowing*, Image Books, 1973.

Jordan, G.   "The Dynamics of Human Longing and the Cosmic
                      Epiphany," unpublished doctoral dissertation, Duquesne
                      University, Pittsburgh, 1986.

Kaminer, W.   *I'm Dysfunctional, You're Dysfunctional: The Recovery
                      Movement and Other Self-Help Fashions*, Addison-
                      Wesley, 1992.

LIVING STRINGS

Kavanaugh, J. — *Following Christ in a Consumer Society: The Spirituality of Cultural Resistance*, Orbis Books, 1981.

Kazantzakis, N. — *Report to Greco*, A. Triadha, trans., Faber and Faber, 1989.

Kelly, G. — *The Psychology of Personal Constructs*, W. W. Norton, 1955.

Kjetsaa, G. — *Dostoievsky: A Writer's Life*, S. Hustvedt and D. McDuff, trans., Macmillan Papermac, 1989.

Knox, R. — *Enthusiasm*, Oxford University Press, 1962.

Kreeft, P. — *Heaven: The Heart's Deepest Longing*, Harper and Row, 1980.

Lambrecht, J. — *Once More Astonished: The Parables of Jesus*, Crossroad, 1981.

Lawrence, Br. — *The Practice of The Presence of God*, Burns and Oates, (1931) 1977.

Lazarus, A. — *In The Mind's Eye: The Power of Imagery for Personal Enrichment*, Rawson Associates, 1977.

Leon-Dufour, X. — "Word of God" in *Dictionary of Biblical Theology*, Geoffrey Chapman, 1967.

Lewis, C. S. — *The Screwtape Letters*, Collins Fount, 1977.

Lewis, C. S — *Mere Christianity*, Macmillan, 1977.

Lubich, C. — *The Word of Life*, New City Press, 1975.

Lynch, W. — *Images of Hope*, University of Notre Dame Press, 1965.

McGuire, B. P. — "The Difficult Saint: Bernard As A Person" in B. P. McGuire, *The Difficult Saint: Bernard of Clairvaux and his Tradition*, Cistercian Publications, 1991.

Maertens, T. — *Bible Themes: A Source Book*, Volume 2, Biblica, 1964.

Maly, E. — "Sin And Forgiveness in the Scriptures" in *Sin, Salvation and the Spirit*, D. Durkin, ed., Liturgical Press, 1979.

Martin, G. — *Reading the Scriptures as the Word of God: Practical Approaches and Attitudes*, Word of Life, 1975.

May, R. — "The Daemonic: Love and Death," *Psychology Today*, I (1968), 16–25.

Merton, T. — *Thoughts in Solitude*, Farrar, Straus and Cudahy, 1958.

— *Disputed Questions*, Harcourt Brace Jovanovich, 1960.

— *The Wisdom of the Desert*, New Directions, 1970.

Miller, M. — "How we Suffer now" in *New York Times Book Review*, May 17, 1992, 44.

Molinie, M. D. — *The Struggle of Jacob*, Paulist Press, 1977.

Murphy-O'Connor, J. — *Paul on Preaching*, Sheed & Ward, 1963.

Murray, J. C. — *The Problem of God*, Yale University Press, 1964.

Muto, S. — *A Practical Guide to Spiritual Reading*, Dimension Books, 1976.

Naess A.   *Four Modern Philosophers*, University of Chicago Press, 1967.

Noel, M.   *Notes to Myself*, H. Sutton, trans., Cornell University Press, 1968.

O'Donoghue, N. D. *Heaven in Ordinarie*, T. and T. Clark, 1979.
Ortega, J.   *The Revolt of the Masses*, W. W. Norton, 1960.
Otto, R.   *The Idea of the Holy*, Oxford University Press, 1958.

Panichas, G., ed. *The Simone Weil Reader*, David McKay Co., 1973.
Percy, W.   *Love in the Ruins*, Avon Books, 1978.
—   *The Second Coming*, Farrar, Straus & Giroux, 1980.
—   *Lost in the Cosmos: The Last Self-Help Book*, Washington Square Press, 1984.
—   "Culture, The Church and Evangelization" in Patrick Samway, ed., *Signposts in a Strange Land*, Farrar, Straus and Giroux, 1991.
Phillips, J. B.   *Your God is too Small*, Epworth Press, 1971.
Picard, M.   *Word out of Silence*, Gateway Editions, 1952.
Pieper, J.   *Happiness and Contemplation*, Pantheon Books, 1958.
Prescott H.F.M.   *The Man on a Donkey*, Eyre and Spottiswoode, 1953.

Rahner, K.   *The Eternal Year*, trans. J. Shea, Burns & Oats, 1964.
Rees, D.   "The Bible in the Life of the Church: An Historical Survey" in *A New Catholic Commentary on Holy Scripture*, Thomas Nelson, 1969.
Reinhold, H. A., ed., *The Soul Afire: Revelations of the Mystics*, Image Books, 1973.
Ricoeur, P.   "Listening to the Parables of Jesus" in C. E. Reagan and D. Stewart, eds., *The Philosophy of Paul Ricoeur: An Anthology of his Work*, Beacon Press, 1978.
Robinson, J. A. T. *Honest to God*, SCM Press, 1963.
Robinson, J. A. T. *The Honest to God Debate*, SCM Press, 1963.
  and D. L. Edwards
Rosenberg, D.   *World Mythology: An Anthology of the Great Myths and Epics*, Harrap, 1986.

Schnackenberg, R. *Christian Existence In the New Testament* (Volume I), University of Notre Dame Press, 1968.
Smart, N.   *Philosophers and Religious Truth*, SCM Press, 1964.
Smiley, J.   *At Paradise Gate*, Washington Square Press, 1984.
—   *A Thousand Acres*, Alfred Knopf, 1992.
Smith, H.   *The Religions of Man*, Harper and Row, 1965.
—   *Beyond the Post-Modern Mind*, Crossroad, 1978.
Smith, M.   *The Word is Very Near You: A Guide to Praying with Scripture*, Darton Longman and Todd, 1989.

Solignac, P.   *The Christian Neurosis*, Crossroad, 1982.
Solzhenitsyn, A.   *Gulag Archipelago III–IV*, Harper and Row, 1975.
Squire, A.   *Asking the Fathers*, SPCK/Paulist, 1973.

Tillich, P.   *The Protestant Era*, J. L. Adams, trans., University of
                        Chicago Press, 1948.
Trémel Y. B.   "Servants of the Word" in *Towards a Theology of the
                        Word: Readings in Theology*, P. J. Kennedy, 1964.
Turner, V. and E.   *Image and Pilgrimage in Christian Culture*, Columbia
                        University Press, 1978.

Unamuno, M.   *The Tragic Sense of Life*, Fontana, 1968.
Underhill, E.   *Practical Mysticism*, E. P. Dutton, 1915.

Vandenbroucke, F.   "New Milieux, New Problems" in L. Bouyer, *A History
                        of Christian Spirituality: The Spirituality of the Middle
                        Ages*, Seabury Press, n.d.
Van Kaam, A.   *The Woman at the Well*, Dimension Books, 1976.
—   *Religion and Personality*, revised edition, Dimension
                        Books, 1980.
Vann, G.   *The Temptations of Christ*, Collins Fontana, 1966.
Vatican Council,
   Second, *see* Abbott, W.

Walker, A.   *The Color Purple*, Washington Square Press, 1983.
Waugh, E.   *The Loved One: An Anglo-American Tragedy*, Little,
                        Brown, 1977.
Weil, S.   *Intimations of Christianity Among the Ancient Greeks*, Ark
                        Paperbacks, (1952) 1987.
Whelan, M.   "Formative Mind I" in *Christian Life Formation*, Part
                        Two, Lecture Nine, Audio Cassette and Notes,
                        Daughters of St Paul, 1985.
—   *The Call to Be*, Society of St Paul, 1986.
Wiesel, E.   *Messengers of God: Biblical Portraits and Legends*, Summit
                        Books 1976.
Wilde, O.   *Oscar Wilde*, editor unknown, Octopus Books, 1983.
—   *The Collected Works of Oscar Wilde*, Collins, 1970.
Wright, G. E.   *The God who Acts*, London, 1952.

INDEX

187

INDEX

Magnificat   133
Mary   129–38, 145
May, Rollo   95
Merton, Thomas   106, 135
Mistrust   118–21
Monty Python   104–5
Moses   37, 156–7
Murray, John Courtney   89–90
Mystery   18, 19, 25–31, 60, 69, 81,
   85–92, 107, 117, 118, 120, 122,
   123, 124, 134–5, 156–7
Myth   26–7, 129–30, 166

New Adam   133
New Eve   133

Ortega y Gasset, Jose   85–6, 100

Paradox   17, 26, 135, 154, 165, 170
Passion   69, 108, 112, 135
Passover   25, 47, 89, 117, 156, 157,
   160
Perception   57, 77–9, 89, 139, 143
Percy, Walker   139–40, 154
Pilgrim Church   134
Pilgrimage   153–64
Pragmatism   121–2
Promise   37, 48, 89, 96, 106, 110,
   118, 120, 131–5, 143, 156–60
Prophets   25, 36–7, 124

Raham   131
Rationalism   16, 79, 129
Report to Greco   145–9
Revelation   13, 14, 15, 27, 89–91,
   156, 160

Ricoeur, Paul   18, 172
Rilke, Rainer Maria   27

Salvation   16, 36, 60, 109, 125, 155–6
Sarah   97, 110–11
Saul   115–28, 149
Schooling   80
Schoomen   2
Sex   39–40, 99–100, 131, 132, 137
Significant people   80
Sin   26, 47, 59, 68–9, 99, 120, 122,
   125, 134
Smiley, Jane   33–4
Squire, Aelred   87–8
Suffering   91, 135, 141

Temperament   80
Thanatos   95
Thanksgiving   43–51
Tragedy   93–101, 107–9, 112
Turner, Victor and Edith   158

Unamuno, Miguel de   101

Valjean, Jean   122–3, 145
van Kaam, Adrian   125
Vatican Council, Second   23, 160

Walker, Alice   75–6
Waugh, Evelyn   104
Weil, Simone   70
Wiesel, Elie   17–18, 110
Wilde, Oscar   53

Zechariah   131, 132, 133
Zephaniah   131, 132–3

189